DELIVERING
YOUR
FUTURE

A CALL TO ABUNDANT
LIFE IN COLLEGE

C. DAVID MORGAN

Praise for the Book

As a father of four, I'm grateful for this compelling book from David Morgan. David draws on his experience and wisdom to provide a valuable resource for students pursuing education after high school. He helps them think through their faith and gifting in a way that is relevant and helpful. I'd encourage all parents to read this book with their teenagers.

Aaron Brockett
Lead Pastor, Traders Point Christian Church

Many books read as though they were concocted in a sterile, research laboratory, Delivering Your Future is NOT one of them. David Morgan delivers a real, 'been there done that' book that offers insight and practical guidance for navigating college.

Todd Wilson
Familyman Ministries

Delivering Your Future is an outstanding book for college students looking for their purpose while navigating the waters of the beginning of adulthood. David Morgan does a phenomenal job of voicing his wisdom on how to find God's calling and meaning for your life. You do not want to miss this read that will be beneficial to your journey through college.

Joe White
President of Kanakuk Kamps

David Morgan takes his readers through a compelling, honest, and heart-wrenching journey in his book Delivering Your Future: A Call to Abundant Life in College. David's book will make you laugh, it will make you cry, and it will help you prepare for the future with courage and hope.

Bill Gemaehlich
Executive Vice President and Chief Operations Officer, Insight for Living Ministries

David Morgan fills a significant need. In Delivering Your Future, he provides a map that helps young people successfully navigate a particularly challenging landscape. Via candor and clarity, he shows that one's faith need not be compromised in college, in fact it can become more vibrant. This is an indispensable guide."

Jack Nikcevich , Regional Director
YoungLife

ISBN: 978-1-7355566-0-4

Printed in United States of America

To My Wife, Sarah.

Thank you for believing the best in me when I couldn't see it. May you ever use your gifts of listening deeply & speaking truth passionately to those you love.

To My Three Sons: Henry, Graham & Blake.

You have what it takes. May this book help guide you and further your understanding of the men God created you to be.

Contents

Introduction

While efficiency and control are the great aspirations of our society, the loneliness, lack of friendship and intimacy, broken relationships, boredom, feelings of emptiness and depression, and a deep sense of uselessness fill the hearts of millions of people in our success-oriented world.

Henri Nouwen

Long before you ever take a college class, you, like many other American teens, are focused on preparing for college. Teachers and parents seem obsessed with the goal of getting their students into the "right" schools. Admission to top institutions is fierce: it takes more work and discipline than ever before to be accepted—not to mention a killer cover letter, a couple of glowing recommendations and a dizzying resume of extracurricular activities.

Preparation for college is starting earlier than ever too. If you're a high school senior, by now you're probably sick of people asking where you're planning to go and what your major will be. But even well before senior year, teachers and parents are already talking about college: advising which AP classes to take, which sports will give you the best chance of a scholarship, and the type of GPA you'll need to be considered at your dream school.

There are countless hours that go into college admission. The mountain of SAT and ACT study guides and endless practice tests you will slowly work your way through. The stomach-churning nerves of test day—knowing your choice of college and potential for scholarships may all come down to a handful of questions. The evenings and weekends spent researching colleges, visiting them, completing applications and writing essays. But then, of course, there's also the thirteen-plus years of schooling you did to even get to this point. All of it leading to that acceptance letter you'll get in the mail. The feelings of joy and relief. That thrill of the first day on campus as you move in. All of the sacrifices and all those years of hard work will have finally paid off.

Getting into a school with good brand recognition, setting out on the right career path, making the right connections with those who will open doors, finding and dating that one person who was made for you, participating in campus life and making memories—all of these things and more are what college is all about. The right school and the right academic preparation: these are the only prerequisites necessary for a great time at college and a good life beyond.

Really? When was the last time you stopped to think about all the hopes you have put into college? What about all the unspoken promises that college will makes you happy? Do you really believe the "right" college can deliver your heart's desires? How can you have an abundant life in college?

Of course, if you've ever attended church—or even Sunday school—you probably already know the answer to this question: college can't give us the desires of our hearts, because only Jesus can do that. However, while we may know deep down that only Jesus satisfies, at the same time our hearts may desperately desire things that are far from Him without even realizing it.

C. S. Lewis illustrates this paradox in his famous series, The Chronicles of Narnia. At the beginning of *The Silver Chair*, Jill is standing on top of a mountain with the lion, Aslan. Far below is the land of Narnia, where Aslan is sending Jill on an important quest. She is to find the lost son of the King of Narnia and bring him home to his father. Jill accepts the task but asks Aslan how it is to be done. The lion then gives her four signs that will guide her along her journey, as long as she pays close attention. When he's finished explaining them, he asks Jill to repeat them back. At first, she doesn't quite remember them, so Aslan has her repeat them over and over and over until finally she remembers them by heart. Then, just before she is about to set out, Aslan gives her one final warning:

Here on the mountain I have spoken to you clearly: I will not often do so down in Narnia. Here on the mountain, the air is clear and your mind is clear; as you drop down into Narnia, the air will thicken. Take great care that it does not confuse your mind. And the signs which you have learned here will not look at all as you expect them to look, when you meet them there. That is why it is so important to know them by heart and pay no attention to appearances. Remember the signs and believe the signs. Nothing else matters.1

Although Jill knows every sign by heart, just as Aslan says, when the signs appear before her in Narnia, not only does she have trouble recognizing them, sometimes she misses them altogether. Why is that? As Aslan warned, "the signs which you have learned here will not look at all as you expect them to look, when you meet them there." A strange reality about people is that we can know a truth by heart, yet not recognize it when it's standing right in front of us. The Pharisees knew by heart every prophecy about the Messiah, yet, when Jesus stood before them in the flesh, they did not recognize Him. This is even more apparent in Luke 7:29–35 just after Jesus encounters John the Baptist's disciples:

"When they heard [Jesus' words], all the people—even the tax collectors—agreed that God's way was right, for they had been baptized by John. But the Pharisees and experts in religious law rejected God's plan for them, for they had refused John's baptism.

"To what can I compare the people of this generation?" Jesus asked. "How can I describe them? They are like children playing a game in the public square. They complain to their friends, 'We played wedding songs, and you didn't dance, so we played funeral songs, and you didn't weep.'

"For John the Baptist didn't spend his time eating bread or drinking wine, and you say, 'He's possessed by a demon.' The Son of Man, on the other hand, feasts and drinks, and you say, 'He's a glutton and a drunkard, and a friend of tax collectors and other sinners!' But wisdom is shown to be right by the lives of those who follow it" (NLT).

The leaders of the day rejected John's non-conventional approach to proclaiming the coming of Christ. You can imagine their thoughts—who is this maverick who lives in the desert and proclaims outrageous and insulting ideas? When Jesus came, He put Himself right in the middle of their culture—reaching those who were ostracized and overlooked. Then the leaders wondered why the son of God would associate himself with these groups instead of their own pious circles.

The end of high school and the beginning of college are often like the high of being on a mountain top. Everything is laid out before you. The air is clean and your mind is clear. College is the quest you've been preparing for your whole life. Your parents, pastors, and teachers have taught you all the skills you need for the journey ahead. But the problem is that as you descend from the mountain top, the "air" will thicken and, if you do not take care, your mind will become "confused." That's because, at college, things will begin to look different than they did at home. Like Jill, the signs you expected to see will not look as you expected them to. This, in short, is the problem of college.

I hope you don't think I'm being melodramatic or some kind of a college killjoy. I had some amazing experiences in college. It was a time of growth and fun, full of many people and memories that will remain with me the rest of my life. I met my wife in college and learned many of the essential skills necessary for me to run many of the businesses I do today. I owe a lot to my time in college. I also have three boys now, all of whom I hope will one day go to college as well. This book is not about discouraging anyone from attending college, nor is it trying to make you feel less excitement about it. It's about the unrealistic expectations we place on our time there. Students do it. Parents do it. Even the church sometimes does it. Whether we realize it or not, we are relying on college to make us happy. College is a great time, but if we rely on it to fill a need that only God can fill, we are setting ourselves up for disappointment.

This book is for young adults on the path to college or at college who might have it all together on the surface, but who secretly wonder what the point is. You know that colleges are selling you a product like anyone else. You're probably aware of the percentage of students who graduate, begin work, then abandon their profession within a few years. Again, people assume that college will make them happy, but often don't realize that it has failed to do so until after it's over. If these sentiments resonate with you, then know that I was one of you as well. If I'm honest with myself, sometimes I still am.

When I headed off to college, I was convinced I had life all figured out. I got into a top-twenty school, developed a system for making straight A's and did not have a hard time finding dates on the weekends. I believed in God, worked out on a regular basis and generally did what I was supposed to do. My plan was to: (1) stay at the top of my class, (2) get a stellar consulting job, (3) work long hours for the first few years after college, and (4) get into a top-tier business school so I could build my own company and become an entrepreneur. If you had asked me about depression or loneliness or struggling with meaninglessness at eighteen, I would have told you something like "those things aren't real" or "you just need to pull yourself up by your bootstraps." But then, that was before the bottom fell out of my life during my junior year of college. What happened? What made a young adult who had a lot of momentum stop in his tracks?

My story is not nearly as uncommon as you might think. Studies show that depression, psychological disorders and even suicide rates are all on the rise in American colleges.[2] This trend can be seen in other places too. In 2018, the British government created a new ministerial position—equivalent to a presidentially appointed post, like the Secretary of State—to tackle the rising epidemic of depression in the UK. This position was titled the "Minister for Loneliness," and immediately many leading news outlets picked up the story with its grim implications for our lives today.[3]

Feelings of desperation and meaninglessness affect millions of students in thousands of locations across our country and our world—young adults today are feeling more isolated and alone than ever before. Most of us probably don't need figures from the "Minister for Loneliness" to tell us that this is true: many of us have seen it firsthand. Here are three recent examples from my own life:

An accomplished business leader, philanthropist, and a good friend told me that his daughter, who had been an honor roll student in high school, was struggling with her transition to college. He and his wife had tried their best to do everything "the right way" with her, but they couldn't find a way to the heart of the problem or to offer any real hope and encouragement. Despite getting into her first choice school with a bright future ahead, the daughter was struggling with feelings of inadequacy and depression.

A colleague, a young mom in her early thirties, provided a second example, when she shared how she went through a period in college when she didn't know which way was up. All the motivation and structure that had propelled her through high school seemed to evaporate after the "newness" of college wore off. She struggled to find motivation or to believe that her future would come together in the way she hoped. As she reflected back on that dark period, she described the approach her friends took to try to help her. One friend attempted to help with some quick advice and formulaic solutions. Although she respected this friend, she felt guilty and ashamed after her time with her. It did little to help her find purpose and meaning. Another friend spent long hours with her and got in the trenches with her—patiently listening and being available to hear what was going on inside her head and heart. She laughed casually when she gave these examples, but then turned suddenly serious, her gaze becoming very focused. "Looking back, I honestly cannot believe how dark my thoughts got at the time. I don't know where my life would have been without that friend." Thankfully her friend helped re-orient her, but many college students do not find such a person. They struggle internally, resisting the urge to let others know they don't have it all together— to let someone into their deepest thoughts and feelings.

Days later, a ministry leader—with twenty years of experience building deep relationships with high school students—shared about how hard it was for him to reach that same level of depth with his own kids. He and his wife had modeled faith their whole lives, but there was just something about spiritual advice coming from parents that made it difficult for their kids to accept anymore.

After hearing these stories, I realized I wasn't alone in my experience of college as a dark and difficult time. Many people who lead accomplished and purposeful lives after college, good people—even strong Christians—went through periods in their lives, often in college, when they struggled with the same questions. They had to take the time to go through the valley, to search the depths and ask the hard questions, before they could come out on the other side and feel like they were on solid footing.

Delivering *Your* Future

My hope for you in reading this book is that it will resonate deeply with some of the hopes you have for college as well as your dreams beyond it. College does not have to be a hard time for you, but if you are relying on it to make you happy—to fulfill the desires of your heart—then you are destined for disappointment and difficulty, like I was.

My hope is that my educational and business experience can help you, the Christian leaders of tomorrow, to identify some of the struggles that might be ahead. Whatever type of college institution you aspire to, I've probably experienced something similar: rigorous Ivy League / top 20 environments (Dartmouth and Vanderbilt), a Big Ten School (Indiana University), and a conservative Christian environment (Dallas Theological Seminary). God has provided some incredible ministry experiences, as well, from working in human resources with Chuck Swindoll's ministry (Insight for Living), engaging with Young Life on local and regional boards, being involved with Kanakuk Kamps and leading junior high and high school groups. Vocationally, too, I've experienced my share: I was an executive in the tenth largest private homebuilding company, worked as a consultant for a Fortune 100 company and have also started, acquired and grown more than a dozen companies. Through sharing my stories and what God has done in my life, I hope you will be better prepared to face the challenges you will certainly face in your own life, whether in college or in your career.

This book, therefore, has three primary parts. The first is about the common hopes and aspirations students have for college. We will explore areas that, on the surface, might seem like good things but can easily lead to problems or sin, if handled carelessly. Some of the truths we will explore may seem basic to those who have grown up in the church, yet Satan has used the same playbook for generations to pull us off track and separate us from God's abundant love and mercy. Just because you know the answers, don't assume these idols and false gods will look like you expect them to at college. *The signs which you have learned here will not look at all as you expect them to look, when you meet them there.*

In the second part, we will explore grounded principles you can cultivate and actionable strategies to avoid the pitfalls of college. These are hard lessons I learned that I hope will help you avoid some of the same mistakes. The final section of the book pulls all of these principles together in practical tools and strategies to find grounding and purpose as you seek to live abundantly through the college years.

While ultimately we rely on God's work in our lives, it is also important that you are not naïve about what you're going to encounter. The challenges are real and the stakes are high, but God promises He will be with you and that He is big enough for any obstacle you may face in high school, college, or beyond. "No trial has overtaken you that is not faced by others. And God is faithful: He will not let you be tried beyond what you are able to bear, but with the trial will also provide a way out so that you may be able to endure it" (1 Corinthians 10:13, NET). Draw courage and hope. God will come alongside of your efforts to recognize and stand up to the siren song you are about to encounter.

Part I: FALSE HOPE

Chapter 1

Get Home

For you have made us for yourself, O Lord,
And our hearts are restless until they rest in you.

Augustine of Hippo, *Confessions*

That feeling when you arrive on campus for your first semester is unforgettable. So much has gone into preparing for that launch; it seems like the culmination of your life so far. The flurry of 'last experiences' in your hometown, the endless goodbyes, the logistics of packing and actually moving to college.

On my first day, my parents and I spent hours carrying in all of my stuff from the minivan and setting it up in my room—everything had to be strategically placed or else it wouldn't fit. We made it through the welcome gathering, opening barbecue, and a variety of other requirements designed to keep us busy. Then the moment arrived to say goodbye. I felt like a pit opened in my stomach as I hugged my mom and then my dad. They got in their car, pulled out of the parking lot, and then I turned and slowly walked back inside.

I sat on my bed and looked around my new room. On the walls were photos of places we'd traveled, milestone events from my life, and other trinkets and souvenirs that were important to me. As I looked, I realized that everything around me was truly a reflection of how my parents had spent the last eighteen years—pouring their hearts and resources into me.

In that moment, I felt a burst of emotions: gratitude ... loneliness ... excitement.

I imagine you will feel something similar on your first day at college too. All those years of late nights and early mornings studying, the barrage of constant deadlines, the list of extra-curricular activities—all of it leading to one goal: getting into the "right" college. For me that meant my dream school, Vanderbilt. As I sat there and reflected on my journey so far, excitement began to overwhelm my other feelings. After all, I had made it—right? This was the destination I'd been working toward my whole life, and now I'd finally arrived. Or so I thought.

Soon, the task of fitting in with a new set of peers was nerve-wracking, and the sheer workload of college was daunting. I plugged into a handful of groups and activities around campus and threw myself into the challenging classes. Enthusiasm, determination and willingness to ask a lot of questions helped me rise to the occasion.

I disciplined myself with rigorous study habits and was rewarded with straight A's my first semester. But this affirmation of success only motivated me to push myself harder and discipline myself even further. I was obsessive in my pursuit of perfection, which extended to a rigorous workout routine, a strict eating pattern, and just enough socialization to meet my needs (and, of course, to make sure I had relevant leadership experience on my resume). All of this behavior was rewarded at college—even praised.

After all, what's not to like about a young man applying himself and succeeding? I rose above difficulties and out-worked my peers. It's the American way, right? Yet in my pursuit of all the "right things," I was quickly becoming unbalanced, or as the Bible would call it, bowing down to idols. Contrary to what you might be thinking, an idol does not have to be a carved image of some ancient god. An idol is anything that captivates our hearts in a way that only God should. Have you ever wondered why the first three of the Ten Commandments are all concerned with our relationship to God?

Exodus 20:3-5 says: "You shall have no other gods before me. You shall not make for yourself a carved image or any likeness of anything that is in heaven above or that is in the earth beneath or that is in the water below. You shall not bow down to them or serve them, for I, the Lord, your God, am a jealous God" (NET).

First, God tells us that He is God. Then He tells us not to create an idol of another god. Finally, He warns us not to bow down and worship these idols of other gods. Surely the Israelites didn't need three commands to tell them not to worship another god? Yet, if we read the Old Testament, we see that's exactly what they needed!

God devotes the first three commandments to who we *should* worship and to what we *should not* worship: this should tell us something vital about the state of our hearts. Every one of us carries the sinful desire to worship things other than God. Christ further emphasized this during his ministry on earth saying that many will hear "*and as they go on their way they are choked with worries and riches and pleasures of this life, and bring no fruit to maturity*" (Luke 8:14). You don't have to physically be bowing down to something for it to be controlling you and consuming your heart.

For me, achievement and approval were my idols, and in college they were easy to worship while still playing the part of a "good Christian." Not only was I great at school, I was decent at socializing, too. Vanderbilt is a college that attracts affluent and intelligent students. My fellow students had been brought up to understand and practice social graces and etiquette. Many of them enjoyed summers at country clubs in between exclusive "camps" around the country. These were not the kids who had spent their high school years studying or working to the neglect of their social image or physical development; nobody rolled out of bed and rushed to class in workout clothes or sweat pants. Everyone devoted great care to their appearance and wore the most popular brands. I was immersed in an environment where everyone looked perfect and acted perfect. Being someone who already loved playing the game of appearances—one who played it without even realizing—this was like adding fuel to the fire.

Even in Christian circles, I found that sins and shortcomings were discussed in a way that seemed authentic but often lacked any grasp of our true sinfulness. We would talk about the theology of sanctification, often engaging in rigorous intellectual debates but it stopped slightly short of calling out our own specific struggles. We admitted our sins to each other, but only the cosmetic ones—the ones that weren't *too* bad.

There was a Vanderbilt alumnus on staff at a popular church, we'll call him Trent. He was a charismatic leader, mature in his theology and experiences. I started attending a study he led with a group of guys. We met at his house and worked through foundational commentaries by theologians like John Stott and John Piper. My intellectual understanding of God grew vastly, but there was never a time when we let down our guard and were vulnerable with each other. I longed, not only for communion with God, but also with other believers.

At one point, Trent encouraged us to fast for twenty-four hours—something I had never really done before. For a college guy, used to roughly four or five square meals a day, this was definitely a challenge! I had never felt more hungry in my sheltered life. At 10:00 p.m. we gathered at a Mexican restaurant to break the fast. Nashville has its share of foodie destinations, but this was definitely not one. Instead, Trent had picked a hole in the wall with red vinyl chairs and menus that were a little sticky. Before we ate, he asked us to go around and share how God had led us in the last twenty-four hours. Some shared specific passages in the Bible, others spoke about clarity God had provided for a relationship or internship, but nobody mentioned anything like the loneliness I was feeling. Nor did anyone bring up binge drinking or specific, honest failings with lust—struggles, I knew for a fact, that we all felt. Regardless, when my turn came around, I quickly came up with similar platitudes about God that fit perfectly within the conversation, but also did not require much deep thought.

Unsatisfied by such superficial connections, I began meeting with Trent one-on-one. During this time, I was candid about my struggles in a way that was beyond my comfort zone but felt good to finally share with someone. Yet only a few meetings later, he told me he was too busy to continue meeting with me. I certainly got it: he was pastoring a church and had a wife and young kids. Still, it was hard not to take this news as a personal rejection. It left me feeling further alone and isolated. As I reflected on our conversation back in my dorm room, I remember thinking I'd lost a good mentor and a friend because I had shared too deeply. It struck me that people might not be able to handle other people's authenticity or messiness, or perhaps they just didn't want to. Frankly, I was not even sure I could handle my own.

I began to implore God for answers. I knew I needed to make a radical change in my life. Good Christians have quiet times every day, right? They (1) wake up early in the morning (2) focus their thoughts on God and (3) Go about the rest of their days led by the Spirit. Each night, I would dutifully go to bed on time so I could get up an extra hour before classes. I would turn on my dorm light and, with a bowl of cereal and an open Bible, I would seek out what God wanted from me. I read a lot, but what I seemed to take away was the good, upright and moral lives that believers were supposed to live; the ability to rely on God to conquer armies, lead troops, and further His kingdom. Somehow, I missed the real and deep laments of David in the Psalms; how utterly comfortable he felt expressing his emotional turmoil and the shortcomings he felt in his life—the times when he struggled to see God at work and the anxiety he felt in his own restlessness. "Search me, O God, and know my heart; test me and know my anxious thoughts. Point out anything in me that offends you, and lead me along the path of everlasting life," (Psalm 139:23-24, NLT).

While David expressed his hurts to God, I avoided them altogether. Often, when I finished classes for the day, I would 'set up shop' somewhere so I could tackle my work for the day. However, before beginning, I would have to intentionally fight to suppress my deep sense that, although I was surrounded by people, not one of them knew me personally or cared anything about me. I forced myself to follow a legalistic formula each day that produced my desired results. This strategy worked for a while ... and then it stopped working. I began to wonder if I needed to change my environment. Maybe I needed to give up on my 'dream school.' Maybe I needed to go to a Christian school or a school closer to home and less prestigious—but then, wasn't that just admitting failure? I was not one to give up easily and transferring felt a whole lot like giving up.

Even so, thoughts of transferring were always swirling in the back of my mind, but one evening they were brought unexpectedly to the forefront while I was on a date. The woman I was out with was gorgeous, godly, and a whole lot of fun to be around. In short, I was very interested. We ate at a Thai restaurant on the outskirts of Nashville (this time it was very much a foodie destination). Over dinner, we shared our dreams and aspirations. By my estimates, it was a near-perfect evening—that is, until we began walking toward her dorm.

She said, "David, I really like you," and my heart nearly beat through my chest. "You are different from other guys I know—in a really good way." Then she paused. "But I have to be honest with you. I doubt I could ever marry a man who studies or works as much as you do. I would always be second to your work." I was completely crushed. I knew this was the woman I wanted to marry. I had dated a lot of girls but she was a different caliber than anyone I'd known before. I also knew she was completely right.

All my outward good works and aspirations were leaving me empty inside—like the Pharisees of Jesus' day who had all the right answers but inwardly were judgmental and proud. I was living up to the external expectations of the world, but in doing so I was not allowing Christ and His deep truths to penetrate to the core of my soul. I knew I had to change, but even though I prayed about it, all I heard from God was silence.

Then one day a few months later, I was returning to campus after doing some volunteer work. I was driving the curvy roads through the Tennessee hills, and I'd just recently read the story of how God spoke to Abraham, clearly calling him to a foreign land. I was pleading with the Lord to give me the direction I badly needed. At that moment, I felt the Spirit prompting me to slow down. I was skeptical. I remember thinking, "*Why should I slow down*?" I needed to get back to campus, and speeding is hardly a big sin. What was the problem with driving fast and praying at the same time? I wasn't exactly hearing some profound revelation that required my full attention. But again, the Spirit spoke to me: "*Slow down now.*"

God had called Abraham to leave his land and later to offer up his son as a sacrifice—yet I was not willing to simply slow down? In a rage, I slammed on the brakes and swerved into the right lane. What I saw next took my breath away. I had pulled behind a large semi and on the mud flaps covering the rear wheels was the phrase, 'Get Home.' Hadn't I been debating whether I wanted to leave Vanderbilt, an environment that was toxic to me, and transfer to Indiana University? Hadn't I known I needed to do something radically different to change the patterns developing in my head? I started to weep. I was overcome by God's graciousness to provide me with clear and specific direction: *Leave Tennessee and get home.*

That the God of the universe would stoop to my level overwhelmed me. I stayed behind the semi for a few minutes before easing back over into the left lane. As I passed, I looked once more. I couldn't believe what I saw. On the side of the truck in bold blue letters were the words 'Delivering Your Future.'

Chuck Swindoll once said that, when God is in something, the pieces fall together. He does not mean to imply that everything will be easy, but rather that, when God intends for something to happen, things seem to work out to make it happen. This was certainly true for me in transferring to IU. Through a family friendship, I was connected with one of the leaders in the business school, who helped me get directly admitted to the honors program at the Kelley School of Business at IU. If not for this small connection, my class credits might not have transferred, which would have prevented me from finishing in four years. It was a small mercy, but one that had a great impact on me: by working in the details, God showed that He was still with me.

Delivering *Your* Future

It seemed as though I was sure to succeed in this new environment. When I started classes, I breathed a sigh of relief: instead of students who were ultracompetitive, with lofty visions for their futures, this student body ran the gamut. In fact, I was soon a little surprised to find there were students at IU who did not care about education at all. Many were simply there to have a good time and extend their college career as long as possible. After the initial 'honeymoon phase' wore off, I began wondering whether moving to IU had been the biggest mistake of my life.

Why had I given up a perfect record at a Top 20 school? Was I really going to have to start building friendships and community all over again? Why had I left the girl of my dreams in Tennessee and moved to Indiana?

The feeling of loneliness that I thought I had left behind at Vanderbilt began to return, but now it felt more like despair. There were upwards of 40,000 students at IU, and I felt more like a statistic than an actual human being. Sometimes I found myself wondering whether there was a single person on campus who actually knew where I was or what I was doing. I felt alone and isolated. My obsession with academic perfection had been my identity, and now it was gone. I felt completely lost.

Christ said, "The thief only comes to steal and kill and destroy; I came so that they may have life and have it abundantly" (John 10:10). I thought the healing process would start as soon as I transferred to IU. I had literally obeyed God's signs, and now I couldn't understand why things seemed to be getting worse. I quickly forgot all the small miracles God had worked in my life to bring me to IU. Instead, I began to doubt and lose faith. *Has God deserted me? Why isn't he sending me any more signs?*

At Vanderbilt, my excessive discipline and drive to achieve had kept me busy, but now I found myself quickly slipping into patterns of sin that I knew were not okay. Like most guys I knew, I struggled with strong feelings of lust. But while I fought against these desires, most of the guys around me chose to gratify their desires as often as possible. They viewed lust as a good thing. They did not understand my beliefs, and I had no one to share my struggles with. I had no community of believers, so I struggled in silence. After giving into my desires, I felt tremendous shame, and as my shame increased so did my propensity to fall into temptation. It was a nasty cycle.

At the same time, I developed an eating disorder with a similar pattern. Food became a source of comfort. When I felt hopeless, I would go to food to find comfort and escape. For the moment, I felt happier. However, soon after consuming a whole pizza or a gallon of ice cream, I would feel really sick and often throw up in an attempt to try to feel better again. To make up for my overeating, I would then resolve to forfeit my next meal. This only made things worse. Even if I managed to keep my promise and skip a meal, I'd get so hungry that once again I'd eat way too much and make myself sick. The cycle of guilt and shame seemed endless.

After months of fighting and losing, I felt exhausted and defeated. I decided it wasn't worth it. Satan convinced me there was no point to my life: my sin ruled my life and I would never be able to escape it. I told myself that I would never be a contributing member of society or an engaged dad or someone who made an impact on the world— I might as well just give up now. So one night I decided to overdose on my prescription pain medicine for migraines.

My despair was so intense that I downed the whole bottle. Immediately, I began experiencing powerful feelings of remorse: What had I done? I knew I was a child of God, how could I let myself fall into such deep despair? I felt lightheaded, but in a moment of clarity, I grabbed my phone and called the one friend I knew would drop everything and come help me.

As I lay on my back looking up at the fluorescent emergency room lights, I wondered how I'd gotten to this point. I'd had every advantage in life: I was from a good home with good parents; I'd grown up going to church and knowing Jesus; I was educated at elite preparatory schools and generally got straight A's; I was well-liked, motivated, and hardworking. When I left high school, I was certain I was fully prepared to succeed in both college and life. Yet, here I was, about to get my stomach pumped after trying to end my own life.

The day after my visit to the emergency room, I called my mom and told her in some vague terms that it might be "good" if they came to "see me." She immediately drove to Bloomington. When she arrived, I was in class and had forgotten that I left the hospitalization paperwork out on a table. My mom let herself into my apartment and found it.

As a father of three kids today, I can only imagine the avalanche of emotions my mom must have been buried under at that moment. Showing up and reading that her son had attempted suicide and yet having absolutely no idea where he was at that moment. It must have been heart-wrenching and utterly terrifying. Seeing the pain I caused my mom was devastating. It was the lowest and most ashamed I've ever felt.

So that's my story—or at least part of it. We will come back to this narrative later on in the book and show how God used even this dark time in my life to mold and shape me. It was not a linear path, and my mom eventually got over the shock of it all and decided she would forgive me, but it took some time. My parents' belief in me and God's ability to work in my life was pivotal. God told me once that my life's purpose is about helping to heal hurting hearts; that's what this book is about.

The world puts a heavy weight on you when your whole future is in front of you. It's really hard to get any perspective; to get to a summit and look around; to taste and see that the Lord is good in the midst of an uncertain and daunting future. Yet, we must get to the summit and take in the view. God created your inmost being, and He has a plan and purpose for your life (Psalm 139 and Jeremiah 29:11). He cares about you greatly and His love for you is infinite. He is not going to give up on you while He's making you into the person you were made to be. God saw me through my college years, and He will see you through your college years too, because with Him, you already have everything it takes.

Discussion / Reflection Questions

1. Do you have a friend or mentor you can be real with about your faith?

2. How can you build deep relationships with others rather than just going through the motions?

3. Can you look back and identify a time when God put the pieces together in your life? Take a moment to praise Him for this.

Chapter 2

Owning a Piece of You

Everything you own owns a piece of you.

Chad Johnson

There are few places anymore where travelers feel totally free from American influence: in Paris, you see the Golden Arches of McDonald's; in Tokyo, students dress like Americans and seek to stay ahead of American and European trends. Don't get me wrong; I love America, but sometimes when I'm on vacation, I'd rather feel like I'm actually in an exotic foreign country instead of an Americanized version of a foreign country! Rural India is one of the few places I've been that seems untouched by the influence of American culture.

On a sunny afternoon, my wife and I rode in an open-top Jeep; the smell of rich earth and clean air refreshing us. The rugged landscape abounded with beauty, with glistening waterways beside soaring mountains. But the real beauty was in the smiles and wonder of its people. My wife is blessed with a gracious demeanor. People are drawn to her caring spirit, and in the villages we toured people crowded around her. They wanted to touch her 'light' hair, to have their picture taken with her and have her pray with them. It was moving for me to watch how she interacted with these people who still live a simple and ancient way of life: farmers who work the land by hand and with oxen, fisherman who shove off in their boats each morning to see what they will catch. Here the rhythms of life are strong, and it's sad that some of this has been lost in our sterilized and insulated modern lives.

Yet amidst this beauty, something sinister lurks—a cousin that is not as easily fooled or hidden. The air was hot and muggy, and my feet quickly became caked in dust. The sound of chanting and bells rang over the land, and the sight of gold trappings glittered in the hot sunlight. As I walked past the temple gates, the sweet smell of incense wafted over me. As I approached the center of the courtyard, I saw a large golden statue: an ancient deity. The sight was startling. It's hard to comprehend from an American mindset. Yet the locals grasp it well. They bow before the image—offering prayers and pleas, bringing their worship, their cares and their wealth to the feet of a statue; an idol that they think will solve their problems and answer their prayers.

This image of a material idol makes the admonition God gave to the Israelites come alive with meaning: "You shall have no other gods before Me. You shall not make for yourself an idol, or any likeness of what is in heaven above or on the earth beneath or in the water under the earth. You shall not worship them or serve them; for I, the Lord your God, am a jealous God" (Exodus 20:3-5). In context of the Israelites worshiping a literal figure made of wood or stone, the concept of idols is as easy to grasp as it is in rural India. People want something to believe in—something they can see and touch. That's why Aaron created the golden calf while the people grew impatient in waiting for Moses to return from Sinai; it's easier to believe in things we can see than those we can't.

The theme of idols is prevalent in the Old Testament as is God's persistence in calling His followers to turn from them. The first act of obedience that God commanded of the mighty warrior Gideon was to leave the idols his father pursued. "Pull down the altar of Baal which belongs to your father, and cut down the Asherah that is beside it; and build an altar to the LORD your God on the top of this stronghold in an orderly manner" (Judges 6:25-26). Before God could invite Gideon into the great work he had planned, He called Gideon to show his allegiance in a way that was visible and impactful. Gideon had to turn away from the idols that had captivated his father's heart and distanced him from devotion to God. Gideon passed the test. He obeyed God completely and quickly: tearing down the lifeless strongholds and raising a place of worship to the Living God. This act would forever change Gideon and reset the course of his life—but it all started with Gideon's recognizing this idol and actively turning from it.

If only it was as clear for us today. If only God would come down and tell us exactly what we need to do in order to be wholly devoted to Him. If only our idols were large, tangible objects that blatantly stood in the face of God, and the whole community around us was literally bowing down to them. It seems like they would be easier to spot—but they aren't. So why is this concept of idols so relevant in our modern context—to a man or woman who is about to head off to college?

An idol is anything you worship apart from God. Andy Crouch, author of *Playing God: Redeeming the Gift of Power*, says that "if your soul is devoted to something that becomes more important to you than God, that is your idol."[1] Idols are things, people or ideas that take preeminence in our lives. They grab our thoughts and vie for our attention in a way that often distorts our perspective and takes our thoughts captive.

Some idols are obviously evil—they are so inherently against our moral codes that they are easy to spot. However, the reality is that most idols are not readily visible. They are not material statues in a temple, but rather desires that lurk in our hearts. There may not be anything wrong with a particular object itself—many of them are actually good things that God wants us to take delight in. Yet, they can wield a subtle power over us that slowly draws us away from God without our even realizing it's happening. In the words of Pastor Mark Vroegop, it's in this moment where "good things" become "god things," and we have created an idol from our own fallen and distorted use. The scary thing is that almost anything can become an idol. Today idols can most certainly be tangible things that money can buy such as clothes, the latest technology, cars, recreational equipment (bikes, skis), or less tangible things like friends, sports, striving for success or beauty, or hobbies. We just don't see them as idols because we don't physically bow down to them. It is the twisting of these things, the obsessing over them, that can distort them and turn our hearts away from the Creator and inward to our own desires and purposes.

Take money for example:

But godliness with contentment is great gain, for we brought nothing into the world, and we cannot take anything out of the world. But if we have food and clothing, with these we will be content. But those who desire to be rich fall into temptation, into a snare, into many senseless and harmful desires that plunge people into ruin and destruction. For the love of money is a root of all kinds of evils. It is through this craving that some have wandered away from the faith and pierced themselves with many pangs (1 Timothy 6:6–10, ESV).

This passage is rich. In writing to Timothy, the apostle Paul encourages him—and us—to be satisfied with the simple things in life: with the food we eat and the materials that shelter us from the elements. He contrasts this with the inordinate desire to be wealthy; to seek the delights of money to the exclusion of other pursuits. His language is direct and fierce: this is a trap which can capture people and imprison them in a vortex of striving that ultimately leads to a wake of devastation. Paul calls out the dangers of money, but take a closer look at the last two sentences; he says that money is *a* root of all kinds of evil not *the* root of all kinds of evil. It can indeed be a force that pulls people away from God, but it is not, itself, inherently evil.

I've been privileged to meet a lot of very successful people. Without a doubt, the people who are the most difficult to be around are those who let their things define them; those who keep chasing after the next thing, who keep running after the next bigger and better deal. It is a stark contrast to those who are also widely successful, but who have a bigger view of life. They have a deep sense of gratitude and appreciation for the things they've been given, but they refuse to let things define them. These people have to push hard against the pull of money and things and lean into God and the people He has put in their lives.

It is really important that you are honest with yourself about the idols in your own heart and keep an eye on them as they grow. The more you give yourself to an idol, the more it will require of you. It's true with any sin really. At first, it's enticing and alluring. You feel a rush of excitement just thinking about it, but the instant you give in, the rush vanishes. The next time you give in to that sin, it will take a little more from you while giving you a slightly smaller rush. Breaking the pattern of sin and idols in our hearts is hard. Crouch says, "Idols may not fail immediately, but they do fail and usually sooner rather than later. Idols almost always disappoint their worshipers."[2] Idols are painfully hard to leave: "Idols do not give up their power without extracting an exit fee."[3]

So how do you know what you have allowed to take a hold over your life? What are the things that are taking you away from being present where God has put you? When I was in college, I attended Christ Community Church outside of Nashville, Tennessee. In one of his sermons, Pastor Scotty Smith said that one of the best ways to identify his own idols was to recognize what his mind focused on before he went to sleep and right after he woke up in the morning. The last thing your mind dwells on for the day and the first thought it goes to in the morning will often hold a clue to what holds your heart fast. I have also found that simply looking at your time and how you spend it can clearly delineate idols in your heart.

As you move toward independence from your parents, what is God calling you to tear down so that, like Gideon, you can give your heart and your life fully to him? As you take this step forward into college—the place that is supposed to set you up for the rest of your life—you will benefit greatly from being keenly aware of the idols you, and those around you, are prone to follow.

Every person is allured by different idols, and the ones that draw you today may not be the same ones that pull you in a different season in life. However, many people develop lifelong patterns of thought and action during college. If you do the work of identifying the idols in your life now, it will serve you well in the future. In the next few chapters, we will explore five idols that will vie for your devotion—at college and as you move into your career: people pleasing, the future, your achievements, your indulgences and your image. These idols may not be as obvious as a golden image found in a remote Indian village, but you can be sure they can wield far greater power over our souls.

Discussion / Reflection Questions

1. Where do your thoughts go when you aren't busy? Perhaps you think, "If only I had _____, then I would be happy." Rather than hiding your idols, bring them to God.

2. Idols aren't always bad things. They are good things that we make into "god things." How do we make sure our hearts love God more than the idols in our hearts?

Chapter 3

People Pleasing

The story of Mary Poppins has delighted children for decades. The premise is simple: Mary Poppins is a wonderful, superhuman nanny who can step into a dysfunctional family—one with distant parents and unhappy children—and through her time with them she can transform and restore their broken relationships. Using a combination of encouragement and discipline, she reorients them to each other and puts their worldly aspirations in perspective.

Walt Disney Studios made the story famous in its 1964 classic movie starring Julie Andrews. Then in 2013, it dove into the real-life backstory in a movie called *Saving Mr. Banks*. It's about the author of the original Mary Poppins book series, a woman named P. L. Travers, and her relationship with Walt Disney, the owner of Walt Disney Studios. Walt wants to turn Mrs. Travers's book into a movie, except she won't let him. Mrs. Travers is a woman who lives her life trying to make up for the void of love she felt growing up with an absent father. The dysfunctional family that Mary Poppins comes to save in her book is therefore a fictional reflection of her own painful childhood. Mrs. Travers's identity is deeply rooted in a father who always let her down, and so she has a difficult time trusting Walt Disney to do a good job telling her story. In one moving scene, Walt pleads with her to let go of the pain: "Don't you want to let it all go? Don't you want to rewrite the tale and let it all go? Forgiveness, Mrs. Travers, is what I learned from those books."[1]

But this isn't just a cute children's story. There are a lot of people who keep seeking "the blessing" from their parents well beyond leaving the home they grew up in. Most of them, like Mrs. Travers, barely even realize they're doing it. It's natural to want to please our parents and often right that we should. Ephesians 6:1 commands children to obey their parents, and Exodus 20:12 commands us to honor them. For many of us, learning how to please our parents is something we have been programed to do from birth. But it can become harmful—even sinful—if it continues to be our primary goal after we leave home. Ecclesiastes 3:1 reminds us that there is an appointed time for everything, and Genesis 2:24 calls us to leave our father and mother when we are joined with a spouse. Pleasing our parents is a good desire, but when it becomes the ultimate desire of our lives, we can find ourselves missing out on the life God intends for us.

This is not an easy thing to balance. In *Saving Mr. Banks*, Mrs. Travers still struggles with wanting to please her father even after he has passed away. She is unable to move past her desire to win her father's approval even if this only ever happens in her imagination. The need for our parents' approval is powerful. It can drive us to all sorts of lengths in the hope of achieving something that is ultimately beyond our control. Like Mrs. Travers, when we base our identity on what our parents think of us, we will always be left wondering if we've done enough.

Pleasing Your Parents

In college and the years that follow, you need to focus on becoming your own man or woman. You should always strive to honor your parents and treat them with respect; after all, their love created you and they likely sacrificed a lot to get you to where you are today. But that does not mean you have to obey their every desire moving forward. You need to start developing the ability to process situations and decisions on your own, without the benefit of having such a direct and constant influence from your parents.

When I was in college, I thought I understood this principle but instead I took it way too far. I hit my senior year in college and was convinced I had to do my job search 100 percent on my own. I refused to even talk with my dad or consult him about the opportunities I was considering. As a result, I landed a job out of college that was not in an industry—or even a location—I enjoyed. It made for a pretty miserable first year post-college. Each morning I trudged to work in the cold and the grey trying to find the motivation to get through the day and accomplish the goals I was given for a job I did not care about. I managed to do it relatively well, and God used the experience to teach me a lot. However, I should have understood that making decisions for myself doesn't mean declining any wisdom or connections my parents might be able to offer. I probably would have landed in a better spot if I had consulted them, but I simply did not understand the difference between obeying my parents and honoring them. I felt like I had to completely shove off.

Have you ever heard the phrase, 'Standing on the shoulders of giants'? It comes from a man named John of Salisbury who in 1159 wrote: "We are like dwarfs sitting on the shoulders of giants. We see more, and things that are more distant, than they did, not because our sight is superior or because we are taller than they, but because they raise us up, and by their great stature adds to ours." What this means for us is that everything we see and enjoy in the modern world—the wonders of science, engineering, medicine and technology—these aren't ours because we're smarter than any generation of humans who ever lived, but because every generation of humans who ever lived has helped us get to where we are by giving us their hard-earned lessons. We can therefore 'stand on their shoulders' and see beyond what they saw.

This is certainly true of our parents. If you are lucky enough to have been born with parents who love, sacrifice for and invest in you, then your whole life will be elevated to a perspective and filled with opportunities that they never had. We can and should benefit all we can from our parents' hard-earned wisdom, knowledge, and even connections without letting ourselves be bound to, or dominated by, their opinions. There is a balance.

It would be remiss for me to leave this subject without a note to those who have come out of childhood with a significant amount of hurt or pain. Even loving, well-intentioned parents can have blind spots. There are certainly also parents who are completely uninvolved or even abusive. If you are coming from any of these places, I encourage you to begin to work through the pain you are feeling. John Eldredge has created a ministry called Ransomed Heart that has a great curriculum and content to help you think through your relationship with your parents and what really drives the hearts of men and women. Often local churches have resources or counseling departments that can help as well. It is worth the time to think through it and seek God's guidance in these situations. Until you get to the root of the problem, the pain you feel will likely continue to affect many of the relationships in your life.

My youngest son has a keen awareness of this that is beyond his years. I came home one night and found him hanging out on his bike in the driveway. I was going for a run before dinner and asked if he wanted to tag along. He agreed and rode alongside me until the end of our neighborhood and then said, "Dad—I don't really want to come on a ride, but I also don't want to disappoint you." To which I responded (in a rare moment of parental clarity), "Henry I just asked because I like being with you, but I will still love you if you don't come on this ride. I understand how a long ride at the end of your day could be tiring. It's okay." He looked at me and motioned for me to come back and then gave me a hug. As I turned to go on my run, he called me back for one more hug. It was a sweet moment of connection that came out of Henry's discernment to honor me without needing to please me. As I headed off on my run and he turned and peddled back to the house, both of us were closer for the clarity and honesty he had provided.

That's a great picture of getting it right: develop an awareness of when you're doing something just to please your parents, so that you can call it out and move forward with the right motivation.

Pleasing Your Friends

The desire to fit in and be accepted is pre-programmed. It's true as early as preschool, and it really does not change later in life. Look at the groups that form in high school around common activities and social settings. In college, this is amplified by the Greek system. Joining a fraternity or a sorority creates an identity that is often helpful in the context of a new school, but which can also threaten you with potentially inordinate pressures to be well-liked, accepted and admired. Depending on the day, fraternities or sororities can be good by providing you the beginnings of lifelong friendships, or challenging by giving you a sense of being better or worse than others based on the social status/current standing of your house.

When I arrived on campus, I was convinced I needed to be in one of the best fraternities. Years ago at Vanderbilt, joining a fraternity happened in the spring semester, so pledges essentially "rushed" the whole fall semester of freshman year. For months, I would head out to parties on the weekends. I spent countless hours making small talk with strangers and inviting girls to come along with me (even though I had little interest in dating them) because I knew being seen with a girl would impress the other guys. I had to ramp up my homework during the week to try and make up for all the time I lost on the weekends. It was a difficult balancing act, and I quickly became exhausted. However, I refused to make trade-offs and instead remained focused on obtaining my goal of getting into the best fraternity. It became my identity. When spring rolled around and I did not get a bid from that fraternity, I was crushed. I felt like I had wasted a lot of time (which was true), and I also felt as though I would never have the social life I needed to be successful at Vanderbilt or anywhere else in life (which was not true). Looking back years later, it's easy to see that I was trying to be something I was not. In his book *Love Does*, Bob Goff says, "I used to be afraid of failing at something that really mattered to me, but now I'm more afraid of succeeding at things that don't matter."[2] I learned a lot through the "failure" of not getting into the house I was set on. I can see now that it would have been pretty detrimental had I succeeded. But I wouldn't flex and look at different houses. I was so hung up on the acceptance I thought I would get from a fraternity that I lost sight of the great friends God had surrounded me with already.

In his spiritual satire *The Screwtape Letters*, C. S. Lewis writes from the perspective of a demon named Wormwood who offers advice to another demon named Screwtape. In one part, Wormwood advises Screwtape to leverage the human desire to please others as a tool to pull people away from God and others: "You should always try to make the patient abandon the people or food or books he really likes in favour of the 'best' people, the 'right' food, the 'important' books."[3] It is easy to get caught up in the idols we think are necessary to our happiness, rather than actually sitting down and prayerfully considering what might bring us a deeper happiness in the long run.

In high school, I had a good friend who always tied her identity to the guys she dated. It was painful to watch. She went from relationship to relationship and never found satisfaction. She was always looking for the next guy that would complete her and make her totally happy. But they never could, because no guy or girl can give us identity if we don't already have it. In college, this cycle is intensified for many people. There is pressure to be in a relationship with someone. In the last year, there can even be a sort of frenzied rush where an amazing number of couples decide to commit to each other right before graduation. I've heard this called "the senior dash" or "the ring by spring," but these are just names different schools give to the same odd occurrence.

Often people come to the end of college and realize they don't have everything figured out like they thought they would. Maybe they always thought they'd meet their future spouse in college and it didn't happen. There is also the pressure of knowing that dating won't get any easier or more convenient in the real world than it was in college. So they hastily pair up with someone equally terrified at the prospect of spending their life alone and they get married. For some couples it works out, for others it doesn't.

In Proverbs, Solomon says, "He who walks with wise men will be wise, but the companion of fools will suffer harm."[4] The people you choose to spend time with in college will affect you either for good or for bad. Having an unrealistic view of them or deriving your self-worth from them will often be encouraged and at times seem natural, but whether it's impressing friends or trying to find a spouse, pleasing others can cause us harm in the long run if we don't pause to think about *why* we want to please these people so badly.

Pleasing Your Network

If you're reading this book, you're probably a pretty motivated individual. When you get to college, it could be tempting to invest a lot of time developing a network that will serve up opportunities to advance in your career. Although this may not be totally apparent in your first years of college, it will become more alluring as you get to the end and especially if you do a graduate program with future high earning potential.

This temptation does not go away later in life either. A few years ago, I was sitting among a group of really high-achieving people, and I found myself dwelling on how their comments and experiences could be leveraged to accomplish my own goals and objectives. I was disengaged with what they were saying and so the meeting lost a lot of the impact that could have been generated during our time together.

Finding ways to align with the interests and opportunities of others can certainly be appealing and beneficial. But as Christians, that is not how we are fundamentally called to approach people. God calls us to love our neighbors as ourselves—to die to ourselves and our own desires for the sake of others. If we aren't careful we can start to view others as a means to an end, rather than as people made in the image of God. This will wreak havoc on your relationships. You will develop a web of superficial relationships that will not be satisfying to you or the people around you because your relationships are built on mutual usefulness, not depth or sincerity.

By nature, we are prone to follow the herd and learn from others. However, if we put our need to please our parents, our friends or our network ahead of wanting to please God, then we will quickly become disillusioned and find we've lost our center in life.

Discussion / Reflection Questions

1. What are some of the good ways you try to please people in your life? What are some the bad or unhealthy ways?

2. We're often worried about what others think of us. What do you think God thinks about you?

3. What do you think his facial expression is when he looks at you?

4. How can keeping our minds on what God thinks of us help us to not worry so much about what others think?

Chapter 4

Your Future Vocation

Be Inspired by Your Surroundings. An education at Harvard has limitless possibilities...You Belong Here. Wherever your life may have started, and whatever its destination, there is a place for you at Harvard.

Harvard College Admissions

During my first semester in grad school at Dartmouth, I was encouraged to begin focusing on interviews. After all, summer was coming up and it was known that you needed to have a phenomenal internship. From that moment on, there was an interview frenzy among students. We were constantly comparing ourselves based on the number of interviews and the quality of our offers. Like many in my class, I thrived on the competition. I was always good at the interview game and soon I found myself on a final round of interviews with a company that was so far from my interests and passions that even an acquaintance spotted it. Yet, I had completely bought into getting the best opportunity I could, and that meant a ton of research, interviews and networking. With all that going on, who has time for self-reflection and asking tough questions? I certainly didn't. The process was exhausting and all my effort was based on fear of my vocational future. I missed out on a lot of life and quality time connecting with my family and colleagues during those years because I was so focused on reining in the best opportunity I could.

Delivering *Your* Future

The claims that colleges make about your future are startling. You have likely worked incredibly hard to get into your chosen college. It was the goal of many well-intentioned counselors to get you focused on this next stage of life years in advance. They had you asking yourself: Where will I go? Who will I become? And what will I do? Trying to answer all these questions about your future vocation can be especially alluring in college, because many of your classes and experiences will be centered on these topics as well. Fear of the future is also brought to the forefront in college, because there is a definite end date and everyone seems to be watching you and measuring how you do. Obsessing over the future can easily take hold of you in a way you don't even realize and meanwhile the world—everyone around you—will applaud your efforts.

Recently, I was coaching a successful executive. We were talking about strategies to help her be more effective in her role as well as wins she had accomplished that quarter. It was a helpful conversation, but I sensed we were not getting to the core issue. Although she was performing well in her role and hitting her goals, she still seemed off—dissatisfied even. Finally, I stopped and took a risk on what I thought was the root problem. She was expecting her vocation to make her feel complete and fully satisfied in life. I told her that no job would ever satisfy her. Not this one, nor any dream job she could imagine. That's because as great as any vocation or job is, it can never love you back. Most jobs will take whatever you are willing to give them. The more you give, the more they will take and you will not even notice it is happening until it might be too late. Even being the head of a growing, successful company doesn't quite fulfill you in the way you might expect it would. There is certainly meaningful and engaging work to be done, but you will be disillusioned and disappointed if you think it will fill your cup entirely.

It is so easy to get hung up on the future: We idolize internships, jobs, vocations, goals and promotions. But when success fails to satisfy in one area, we dream up another where—this time—we're certain we will finally be satisfied. The truth we need to understand is that trying to find satisfaction in the future will keep you on a never-ending search for something that is always just beyond your grasp, like chasing a rainbow that is perpetually just over the next hill.

Discussion / Reflection Questions

1. Worry doesn't end after you begin your vocation. How can you begin to trust God with your worries now?

2. Think for a moment about the vocation you think God might be calling you to. Now imagine that after college God suddenly calls you to something completely different. How would you react? Would you still trust Him?

3. One of Stanford University's mottos is, "The Wind of Freedom Blows." How does this hit you as you think about your own expectations around where college will get you?

Chapter 5

Your Achievements

I know a wheel is starting to fall off when the meal I'm preparing becomes more important than the people I'm preparing it for. When my work becomes more important than the family I am working for. When a point I'm making becomes more important than the person I'm making it to. That's how I can tell I've lost my axis. When I lose sight of what's more important. When I lose a sense of sacredness of another human being.

Ken Gire, *Windows of the Soul*

A couple of years ago on a beautiful fall morning, I made my debut as a coach of my son's soccer team. The league stressed that six year-olds weren't playing to win; they were playing to have fun. This was a recreational league, they said, designed purely to foster a love of the sport. That's all well and good, but somehow the kids on my team didn't receive this message. After every goal, they cheered, high-fived, and congratulated each other on our rising score and the other team's lack thereof. This continued throughout the game (and it's possible I even encouraged it at one point) until finally the other coach intervened. He was visibly frustrated, and for some reason he did not find my team's competitive spirit very funny (it might have had something to do with the fact that his team was losing—by a lot), and so he tried to get the kids to stop keeping score. He did not succeed. Even at age six, there is an innate desire to keep score—to compete.

The desire to compete—to accomplish, be the best, come out on top—is bred into us from an early age in our culture. And that certainly isn't all bad. Keeping score can be good, as can setting goals and achieving them. Like anything else, achievements become bad when our thoughts become consumed by them; when we measure ourselves by our achievements and constantly compare them to others.

In college, the most obvious form of accomplishment is academic success. The desire for good grades or that perfect 4.0 can soon become something that consumes you. The problem is made worse because everyone around you will praise you for it, which makes it far easier to bow to this idol without having the faintest idea that you're doing it.

When I was at Dartmouth, a notable alumnus addressed our class. He was quite successful and most people in the room were silently coveting his job as he spoke. When asked for advice about how to do graduate school effectively, he said that he wished he had studied a little less and taken the time to get to know his classmates a little more. He thought he had to be at the top of his class to accomplish his goals in life, but looking back from a few years away, he realized that the relationships he developed had propelled his career more than his academic success.

Another time, the faculty at Dartmouth openly encouraged us to move away from an exclusive focus on academic success. During our orientation, the dean sat us down and told us we were about to go through the hardest and most intellectually challenging experience we would ever go through. Before it started, they wanted us to realize that we were all used to being top of the class, but the faster we moved past the desire to be at the top, the more collaborative and impactful our experience would be in graduate school. When he'd finished, I looked around the room and everyone else looked about as stunned as I felt. Mouths gaped and eyes were wide. We could not believe what we were hearing. Until that moment, we'd all worked diligently to boost our grades and resumes to get into all the various programs along the way to Dartmouth. The idea that we should now collaborate, rather than compete, seemed crazy. That the dean of the school was actually *encouraging* this was too much for most people.

Your college program probably isn't going to start with a plea to get along. It will be hard to maintain perspective in the midst of a highly pressured academic environment—especially one that is hard to get into. You will be encouraged to get caught up in the focus on academic success to the exclusion of everything else in your life. It will be easy to follow along. The problem with academic success is not that good grades are bad, but that it is easy to measure your own self-worth solely based on what grades you're getting. This can lead you to spend four years pouring yourself into achieving a 4.0 without ever stopping to question whether that's actually the target you want to be aiming for.

In the 2004 Athens Olympics, American Matt Emmons was on track to win gold in rifle shooting. He'd devoted the majority of his life to becoming the very best at his sport, and now he was poised to fulfill this dream. Across the globe, millions of people watched as he prepared for his shot with automatic precision. His stance was flawless and his concentration was intense. He squeezed the trigger and the rifle fired. When he looked up, he saw a bullet hole just where he'd aimed it—in the very center of the bullseye. It was a perfect shot. The only problem was that his bullseye was on someone else's target. Emmons had literally aimed for the target next to him instead of his own. He landed a perfect shot, but a perfect shot on the wrong target counts for nothing. He was awarded zero points and lost the medal he'd been training for his entire life.

Bob Goff used this illustration at a men's group I attended. It's a common reality for many of us. We find ourselves running after the wrong target—comparing ourselves to someone else's target instead of our own, and finding ourselves coming up short. In

Bob's words, "Comparisons are what keep you from being who you really are."[1] Our idols have a lot to do with comparisons. They lure us into a vision of who we could become or what we could be like. They promise that if we achieve this or distinguish ourselves by doing that *then* we will finally feel worthy. The trouble is that these promises are lies. The only way to feel worthy is by understanding, believing, and living in the reality that God the Father loves us—not because of any achievement of our own—but because He sees each of us as if we lived the perfect life and died the perfect death that Jesus achieved for us. Achievement feels good in the moment. It is part of the way that God has made us. But be careful that accomplishing goals and getting good grades is not satisfying you by making you feel better than those around you. In the end, comparison based on achievement will lead you on an unending journey of proving yourself. You may shoot bullseye after perfect bullseye, but are you aiming at the right target?

Discussion / Reflection Questions

1. Think of the most successful person you know. What attributes or achievements made you think of them? How do you think they define success?

2. Why do we want to be successful? What does success do for us?

3. How does God define success? Who is someone you know that is successful by God's standards, not the World's?

Chapter 6

Your Indulgences

Eat drink and be merry for tomorrow we die.

George Jacques Danton, Leader in the French Revolution

The free for all, right? That's what college is all about. Being able to experiment and explore all the things you wanted to in high school but could never quite get away with in your parents' house. You can control your class schedule, pick your friends, determine your living situation, attend parties and date around. Plus—one way or another—most of your expenses will be covered, either by your parents or deferred debt, so chances are you may not even have to worry about supporting yourself. You're free to enjoy yourself to the fullest without anyone watching over your shoulder.

A friend of mine once told me about dropping off his son for freshman year at college. He and his wife were saying goodbye and wishing him well when his wife unexpectedly stepped out of the car to retrieve one last item: a mega pack of 100 condoms. She completed the drop off by saying, "Look, I don't really need to know what you do while you're here, but just make sure you don't get a girl pregnant because it will ruin your life." The husband told me he was a little shocked at her parting words and the quantity of birth control she thought would be needed, but surprisingly he did not counter her. They accepted the fact that their son had freer rein than ever: they were just being realistic and helping him be prepared.

Delivering *Your* Future

Many people approach college this way, as a time to explore and experiment because the rest of life will be about responsibility and productivity. If you allow yourself to follow these patterns, they certainly seem satisfying in the moment. I had a fraternity brother at Indiana University who was a perpetual senior. We genuinely did not know if he was on his second or third senior year. It was the subject of great folklore around the house. He was good-natured and liked to joke, but what was going on just below the surface was a little concerning. Indulgence and instant gratification ruled his life and left him in a cycle of repetition that was slowly moving him further from graduation and further into debt. I felt bad for him, because in my own way I could relate to him.

When I was in high school, I was heavily influenced by the guys around me. They often boasted about their exploits with girls (whether real or imagined), and I decided that to be accepted by them, it was time I started pursuing girls. My beliefs often kept me from going too far, but I could still talk about the girls I was spending time with in a way that was relevant to the guys I wanted to impress. This seemed like enough to gain their approval while also remaining relatively harmless. The problem was that I did not really like some of the girls I casually dated. I was using them, at first for approval, and then because it made me feel important. Although the girls were certainly willing participants, deep down I felt horrible because I knew I was using them to feel good about myself and to accomplish what I thought I needed to do to be accepted by others.

Maybe you've had success in defeating lust in the past. Maybe you were like me in high school and carefully flirted with the line between harmless fun and sexual sin without too many problems. But college is a time of more autonomy and less accountability. If you have had success in defeating sexual sins or lust in the past, it might be tempting to think you're beyond it and don't need to worry about it anymore. The moment you think you are above sexual sin is likely when you're most vulnerable.

Second Samuel 11 describes King David's infamous fall into sexual sin. Let's keep in mind that David was likely in his fifties when this happened—an accomplished general and a respected king.

Then it happened in the spring, at the time when kings go out to battle, that David sent Joab and his servants with him and all Israel, and they destroyed the sons of Ammon and besieged Rabbah. But David stayed at Jerusalem. Now when evening came David arose from his bed and walked around on the roof of the king's house, and from the roof he saw a woman bathing; and the woman was very beautiful in appearance.

Instead of being out on the battle lines with his men, David stayed behind. He was likely bored and restless. Chuck Swindoll described it well when he said, "David was in bed, not in battle. Had he been where he belonged—with his troops—there would never have been a Bathsheba episode. Our greatest battles don't usually come when we're working hard; they come when we have some leisure, when we've got time on our hands, when we're bored."[1] As David walked around his roof on a warm Jerusalem summer night, his eyes saw a woman who captivated him, and as the king, he decided he must have her. It's important to realize that the Bible calls David a man after God's own heart. He was someone who had seen God deliver him in miraculous and un-expected ways. His faith was real and strong. Yet, he still fell prey to this basic carnal desire, and it wreaked havoc in his life and the relationships most important to him.

Don't be naïve going into college: while some are more susceptible than others, no one is above sexual sin. There will be a very real battle that will take place in your heart, and a lot of it will be fought through desires of the flesh and indulgences. Now, a lot has been written and preached about sexual purity over the years and not without reason. But let me be clear, it's not that sexual sin is worse than other kinds of sin; it's not. It's not that God cannot forgive and heal sexual brokenness; He certainly can. God's grace is more than enough to cover all kinds of sin. Sexual sin is not worse, but it can be an everyday, common, and perpetual struggle. Resistance can often seem pointless, yet giving in and indulging your desire can pull your heart away from God at an alarming pace. Paul points this out really directly in 1 Corinthians 6:18 when he says, "Run from sexual sin! No other sin so clearly affects the body as this one does. For sexual immorality is a sin against your own body" (NLT). We will circle back to this topic later in the book, but for now it is enough to acknowledge how strong a pull this can be when you are unchecked and unguarded in this area.

Discussion / Reflection Questions

1. What do your non-Christian friends think of sex? What is God's design for sex? What are the similarities or differences in these views?

2. Do you think God really cares if you use your body as a playground to have fun? Why do you think that?

3. Should we feel shame and isolate ourselves from God when we mess up? What should our reaction be when we fall into sexual temptation?

Chapter 7

Your Body Image

Or do you not know that your body is a temple of the Holy Spirit who is in you, whom you have from God, and that you are not your own? For you have been bought with a price: therefore glorify God in your body.

1 Corinthians 6:19-20

In a sermon, New York City pastor Timothy Keller commented that we are more image conscience now than we have ever been in the past. We are absolutely starved for images. Texting takes too long. Now we just send a photo instead of taking the time to write something out.[1] C. S. Lewis lived in a time that was far less image-conscious than the present, yet he also talks about how our perception of beauty and the ideal body image are largely determined by the culture around us—and always have been. Hundreds of years ago, beauty was epitomized by pale skin and a slightly chunky figure (both for men and women!). Coincidentally, being pale and plump were also two indicators of great wealth; only the rich could avoid working outside and only the rich had access to enough food to overindulge at the table. Because these qualities were rare, people considered them beautiful.

This may sound comical to us from our current cultural lenses, but when you think about it, the same is still true today. We may think tanned skin and a toned body are beautiful—but why? Tanned skin means that you can either afford frequent vacations to warm locations or it means you spend lots of money on tanning beds. A toned body means you eat fresh, healthy foods, rather than fast food. It also means you frequent the gym or hire a personal trainer in your free time, rather than working the second shift to pay bills. In other words, the things that we think are "beautiful" are actually still just things we can create if we have enough money. Our modern ideal of beauty may look very different from old fashioned ones, but underneath we haven't changed a bit.

Lewis believed that this perpetual chasing after whatever traits or attributes are in vogue at the time is exhausting and misdirected. "As a result, we are more and more directing the desires of men [and women] to something which does not exist—making the role of the eye in sexuality more and more important and at the same time making its demands more and more impossible."[2] Isn't that so true of us? Lewis wrote those words in 1952, but they sound as if they were written last week. When looking good could require plastic surgery, tanning beds, diet pills, photo filters, and daily sessions with a personal trainer—not even our celebrities can live up to the impossible images they post. The images of perfect bodies we see on social media and in magazines simply aren't real. Yet somehow the impossible still becomes our standard, and we feel guilty when we can't match it.

You've probably noticed a trend with these idols by now, and body image is no exception: in college, the tendency to compare our physical appearance to those around us is intensified and exaggerated. A professor of mine actually called out in class one day, "Just wait until the middle of February ... after you've all been staring at each other for hours on end in classes and at social events, and you are all stressed out about where you will land for the summer. That is when school really gets tough." And as I went through the term, I realized he was right: We were constantly comparing ourselves with our peers in terms of physical appearance, job progress, and academic success.

The toxic thoughts that spring from an over-emphasis on physical appearance can often push people to pursue destructive behaviors in an attempt to correct them. One study that is cited frequently showed that "eating disorders among college students surveyed from one college increased from 7.9 percent to 25 percent for males and 23.4 percent to 32.6 percent for females over a 13 year period."[3] Another more recent study suggested that "20% of respondents said they suspected that they had suffered from an ED at some point in their lives."[4]

Did you catch that? Eating disorders are prevalent in *both* men and women. When we don't feel thin enough or beautiful enough, the guilt we pour onto ourselves actually causes us to form unhealthy relationships with food. Rather than solving the problem, we accelerate it. This is a common pattern of sin associated with guilt and shame. These emotions, far from freeing us from our sin, actually serve to further enslave us to it.

In her popular book *The Hunger Games,* Suzanne Collins writes of a world that has been manipulated and controlled in order to benefit those with greater beauty and wealth over the poor and plain. The beautiful live in decadent cities and the plain live in squalor and are forced to do manual labor for the beautiful. In a particularly memorable scene, Collins describes an opulent party in the wealthiest quadrant. The food is completely over the top: an extraordinary buffet appealing to all the senses. The guests gorge themselves until they are stuffed. Then they are served a brightly colored chaser which causes them to quickly surrender their recent indulgences to the porcelain throne—or in other words, to vomit into the toilet.[5] Despite everyone's obsession with beauty, indulgence and greed are encouraged even when the results are revolting. Although this scene is certainly an exaggeration, the reality is still not too far from how our society behaves—on college campuses especially.

In an environment full of changing schedules, transient relationships, worry about the future, pressure to perform and constant competition, food becomes one of the easiest ways to find reliable and quick relief from stress. We call certain foods "comfort foods" for a reason. Indulging in food that reminds you of home or that is full of sugar and other unhealthy ingredients is a distraction from pain and stress like anything else people might seek to distort the reality they face.

What you eat and how much you exercise can be among the few things you are able to control in your life. For some people, their bodies are the one thing they can exert mastery over. It's easy to pull the reins in on food when other things seem out of control, to get obsessive about counting calories and working out. With the increased pressure to be in a relationship, this can quickly become as enslaving as an eating disorder. Your day may revolve around your workout schedule. If forced to skip a workout one day, you may become irritable and insecure. I struggled with this in college. I became obsessive about working out—often not feeling whole or complete that day if I had not worked out or if my workout was not hard enough. Depending on how I felt about my workout, I would alter my eating, often skipping meals or eating too little. But this threw me into a pattern of working out, then eating too much, sometimes throwing up, and then repeating it again. It became a vicious cycle. I never felt good about myself and the cycle seemed to increase my despair. While there is nothing wrong with wanting physical exertion, if your outlook and attitude toward yourself is largely affected by it, the benefits become destructive.

Like any addiction, an obsessive focus on your physical appearance or your food intake can become lonely and isolating. You often feel as though you are the only person who struggles with this. That is when the negative thoughts begin to repeat in your mind—whether by your doing or the enemy's.

In the movie *Collateral Beauty*, Will Smith portrays a successful entrepreneur who completely loses his way when his daughter dies tragically and unexpectedly. He loses all sense of purpose and direction. Finally, he starts attending a group with other parents who have lost children and discovers that he is not alone. There are others who have the same sense of hopelessness and lack of motivation every day. This realization, far from depressing him further, is the thing that sparks his healing. Isolation is a breeding ground for foolishness. The more you keep to yourself and do not let others in on your struggles, the greater the chance you will fall into destructive thoughts and behaviors. Open up about your struggles to a trusted friend, a pastor, or a family member, and things will seem far less hopeless than they did before.

The Bible says that God designed each of us with unique physical attributes. It also says that if we are Christians then our body is a temple of the Lord. This is not a metaphor. As Christians we believe that the Holy Spirit literally lives inside us, that our body is his dwelling place and that it is our job to pursue holiness. Knowing that our own physical bodies are a temple to the Lord can be both motivating and daunting at the same time. Delighting in a table spread with food at Thanksgiving can be honoring to God, and running an ultra-marathon can be honoring to Him. But when the appearance of "the temple" becomes more important to us than the Spirit that dwells within, then we know we're off track. First Samuel 16:7 says, "For God sees not as man sees, for man looks at the outward appearance, but the Lord looks at the heart."

Some questions you might ask yourself in regard to your body image could be: How do I honor God with the choices I make while also not becoming obsessive about it? Where is the balance between taking time to take care of myself and not letting appearance consume me?

Discussion / Reflection Questions

1. Do you feel comfortable and happy with your body or do you feel as though there is room for improvement? Do you think that having a perfect body would make you happy?

2. Is there a balance between being fit and having an image obsession? What is that balance?

3. What do you think God thinks about the body? Is it good or bad?

Chapter 8

The Mirage

[God] relies on troughs even more than on the peaks; some of his special favorites have gone through longer and deeper troughs than anyone else.

C. S. Lewis, *The Screwtape Letters*

Universities today are marketing experts. They want to convince you that they will provide all the freedom, opportunity and connections you possibly need to set you up for the rest of your life. The rankings, highly-targeted websites, and motivated admissions staff all work to create an aura of unquestionable trust in their system.

For the purposes of this chapter, I'm going to call all these schemes, promises, and rankings "the mirage." In folklore, a mirage is a vision travelers in the desert sometimes see. When they become severely dehydrated, their eyes begin to play tricks on them. They're certain they can see fresh water springs in the distance, but as they come closer, to their dismay, they realize it was just their desperate mind seeing what it wanted to see. This is a good image of what college is like: We're so desperate for success and future security that we readily believe those who assure us that they can provide it. For many students, universities do offer a gateway into a career path and the skills needed to progress, but the challenge for believers is that we are called to a deeper meaning and a more significant purpose than just advancing our vocations or achieving status and wealth in life. What follows is a list of some of the things you might find in truth/reality instead of the marketing mirage.

The academics will be harder than you expect.

Good colleges will challenge you to manage your own time, chart your own course and figure out how to succeed on your own. For many, this is very different from the hand-holding they experienced in high school, even for those who went to college-prep high schools. College is a different level. You can have a class at 10:00 a.m. on Tuesday and not have another one until Wednesday at 3:00 p.m. It will be up to you to figure out how to best use all that time in between. I will never forget one of my graduate classes when they had us buy all of the books for the semester, but did not help us at all with a reading plan or any kind of a breakdown on how to get it accomplished. You could literally leave it all until the last week of the semester. Nobody was checking along the way to see if you were doing what you were supposed to: The responsibility was all on you. Some people excel with this sort of freedom to manage themselves, but I think most of us find it quite an adjustment.

You will feel lonely.

Prior to college, your life was spent in some type of family environment. You may not have had the picture-perfect family—no one does. All families have their idiosyncra-sies and dysfunctions. However, moving from your family home to the college dorm means that—one way or another—you are moving from a location with a system of support to a location without one. Perhaps until this point, your relationship with a sibling has been love-hate, but nevertheless, you know your sibling would be there for you if you needed him or her.

I'll always cherish the way our boys would act when they were reunited after being apart. At first they had liked the space from one another, but inevitably they would start asking what their brother was up to and when he was coming back. When the brother finally returned after being at camp or wherever, they gave each other the goofiest looks. It was as if they were trying not to smile despite being completely delighted to see each other. Then they would begin roughhousing and wrestling like bear cubs. Although they fought often when they were younger, they loved each other and knew they had a counterpart who would always watch their back. This sort of bond and loyalty is a given in most families—even among siblings with less than friendly relations.

At college, this sort of community can't be taken for granted. The relationships you formed at home took years to establish. When you arrive at college, you may not know anyone. You are going to have to start over again. For some people, this comes really naturally—especially to those who play sports or have a strong appetite for extracurricular activities or who are naturally outgoing. However, for most it takes a bit of work. Although making acquaintances to eat lunch with or sit by in class is fairly easy, making friends—true friends, who love you and will watch out for you—is a much more difficult task. One that takes time and effort from you and from them.

You may come out with more questions than answers.

This one is particularly scary because few people think about it before going to college. College is where we go to learn answers about the world and about ourselves. It is lauded for this. A good college will certainly provide that opportunity, but it won't—and can't—answer all your questions. Like anything in life, college is what you make of it, or you will get out of it what you put into it. Hopefully, it will provide you with a good starting point, but don't put too much pressure on yourself or onto your college years to have it all figured out. Your goal should always be to find the next step and take it—you have the rest of your life to figure out the rest.

No one is going to hold your hand.

That's right—if you don't wake up to your alarm, mom is not going to be there to make sure you get to class. It's up to you. For some reason, professors are not generally very sympathetic to students who consistently miss their classes then complain later about not getting good grades. Also, as good as the placement offices are for jobs, it will ultimately be on your shoulders to get it done. They can have the best interview guides ever, but you still have to do the prep work to think about the questions that will showcase your abilities and highlight your talents. No one can do it for you.

Additionally, you may be surprised at how many things happen in life because of who you know. It is actually pretty normal. Think about it—if you have a choice to go on a spring break trip with friends you know well versus taking a trip with people you have never met, you would pick the trip with people you know. It is the same way with jobs and careers. If someone you know and trust refers a candidate for a job opening, it is just human nature to talk with that person first because he is recommend by a trusted source.

There is a good chance you won't sleep well.

I remember one evening during my first few weeks when I had my first exam the following day. After cramming the last bits of information I could, I went to bed at—what I thought was—a reasonable time, around 11:30. It turned out that my next-door neighbor in the dorm did not have an exam the next day and saw no need to turn his music down. In fact, he had invited a few friends over to enjoy the late evening with him. Frustrated, I got out of bed and asked him to turn it down (a little dorky, I know). As you might imagine, I did not get a lot of sympathy from him. And guess what? It happened again and again. I finally got to the point where I just accepted I would go to bed at 2:00 a.m. every night and stopped trying to fight it.

Now, you might be thinking this sounds glamorous: no parents to impose curfew on you and the ability to stay up as late as you want. And it is fun—for a while. That is until you start to get completely exhausted and everything seems to be a bigger deal than it is because of your lack of sleep and inability to think clearly or stop and rest.

You may have feelings of discouragement.

At some point you probably will get discouraged. For some, discouragement can lead to thoughts of self-harm. "About 7 percent of students nationally report having experienced suicidal thoughts in the last 12 months, statistics show. About 1 percent attempt suicide. For Penn, a school of 24,000 undergraduates and graduates, that would translate to 240 students."[1] It is a hard environment, and if you go in unprepared or are surprised when you find you have these feelings, it will not make it any easier to walk though.

I was at a funeral a few years ago of a respected leader in our community who had committed suicide. I was struck by what his widow said in her remarks: "He simply did not weather storms well." This leader could not see his way out when dark times came and challenges loomed ahead. In other words, he had lost hope, and the result was a sudden suicide that confounded his family and sent shock waves through the whole community. He kept his negative feelings to himself and didn't ever let anyone else in.

You may come out of college in debt.

Many students take on significant debt in college. It's how the system works these days. It puts you in a position of pressure to find work, if for no other reason than to satisfy the looming debt and interest payments. Debt puts people in a tough situation, and the cost of education is still rising rather than falling, making debt a reality for the majority of students. It will be important to be as smart as you can about the resources you have to work with in college. Even if your parents or grandparents help you by paying for some or all of your education, you will likely still come out with a sense of obligation to "repay them by making good on their investment."

Conclusion

The chances are good that you will experience three or more of these realities in college. Dallas Willard says, "The most important thing in your life is not what you do; it's who you become. That is what you will take into eternity."[2] That is pretty easy concept to grasp, but a really hard one to internalize. God is about what you become, the character you are developing, the way you take delight in Him. In college, He is going to use you to impact others for Him and help you develop into a man or woman after His own heart. It simply is not about you or your accomplishments.

The way of the world is our natural default. Following the way of God takes constant effort, thought, and help—from others and from God. C. S. Lewis described it like this: "It comes from the very moment you wake up in the morning. All your wishes and hopes for the day rush at you like wild animals. And the first job each morning consists simply in shoving them all back; in listening to that other voice, taking the other point of view, letting that other larger, stronger, quieter life come flowing in. And so on, all day."[3]

It all starts with having a deep grounding in hope and purpose despite the daily struggles and pressures. A strong belief that God is at work in your life and will bring about his purposes. As Paul describes in Philippians 2:12 -13, "So then, my beloved, just as you have always obeyed, not as in my presence only, but now much more in my absence, work out your salvation with fear and trembling; for it is God who is at work in you, both to will and to work for His good pleasure." These verses bring a deep sense of hope that in spite of the chaos and uncertainty of the world around us, God is still active and alive in our lives. Every experience, every interaction, every thought has the opportunity to pull you closer to Him or to pull you away.

Discussion / Reflection Questions

1. How will you acknowledge that these struggles are a part of the college experience while still remaining present during your time there?

2. What do you think will be the idol you will struggle the most with and why?

3. How can you ask God for his power and grace for dealing with this idol?

4. How do you encourage and give grace to those around you who are likely struggling with the same issues, even if they don't recognize or admit it?

PART II: ILLUSTRATED HOPE

Chapter 9

Illustrated Hope

The true soldier fights not because he hates what is in front of him,

but because he loves what is behind him.

G. K. Chesterton

In *The Giver*, Lois Lowry describes a world that seems to have perfected hope. The characters live in a utopian society of peace and harmony, but the tradeoff is that it is devoid of individual freedom.[1] Residents of the city take pills every day to keep their emotions in check, and the leaders carefully think through each child's abilities to direct them to a vocation. Childbirth is even replaced by a sterile, utilitarian experience. The weather is always perfect and no one lacks food or clothing. The only problem is that one person has to know the truth. The Giver is tasked with preserving information about humanity that is both good and bad. He has to remember what happened before and help guide society so it does not destroy itself in its effort to create perfection.

The hero of the story is Jonas, a boy being trained to be the next Giver. As he learns, he awakens to the reality that there has to be more out there. His current sense of hope is derived from doing what he has been instructed to do: to not think too much and to enjoy each empty and purposeless day. Jonas also discovers that emotions are things you feel and that they can be used for good and not just evil. This flies in the face of the lie he had been programmed to believe that emotions were bad and should be neutralized and managed at all costs. At a pivotal moment, it seems that all hope is lost. Jonas desires to live holistically in truth, but the obstacles seem insurmountable. Then he has a vision of a home covered in snow and decorated for Christmas. He hears the carol "Silent Night" playing. This is the ultimate symbol of hope for Jonas. Suddenly the obstacles don't seem as impossible as they did moments before, because Jonas remembers what he is fighting for. Jonas does not know what the future will be like, but he has a sense of hope and that hope motivates and sustains him.

In *The Lion, the Witch and the Wardrobe,* C. S. Lewis depicts a world that is far from the Utopian society in *The Giver.* The land of Narnia is ruled by the evil White Witch and also under a curse that makes it always winter but never Christmas; life is always hard but without that small vision of hope that Jonas glimpsed during his struggle. However, beneath the surface of Narnia there is a deep, hidden hope: there is a prophecy that one day Aslan, the lion, will return to Narnia and rid it of perpetual winter and the White Witch. This prophecy seems to have been fulfilled, until the White Witch kills Aslan at the Stone Table.

Even though he is not outmaneuvered or overpowered, Aslan gives himself up to the Witch. He agrees to die in the place of a traitor in his army, a boy named Edmund, who fell prey to the lies and false hope of the White Witch. As a result, Aslan offers his life as a sacrifice to save Edmund—a substitution that the White Witch is all too happy to accept. Edmund is nothing to her, but Aslan is her great enemy. Edmund goes free and Aslan turns himself over to be executed. The Witch and her army put Aslan to death at the Stone Table. With Aslan dies the hope of all Narnians, except that Aslan knows something that no one else does, a Secret about the world that the others—even the Witch—has failed to grasp. Here's how Lewis puts it:

At that moment they heard from behind them a loud noise—a great cracking, deafening noise as if a giant had broken a giant's plate. … The Stone Table was broken into two pieces by a great crack that ran down it from end to end; and there was no Aslan.

"Who's done it?" cried Susan. "What does it mean? Is it more magic?"

"Yes!" said a great voice from behind their backs. "It is more magic."

They looked round. There, shining in the sunrise, larger than they had seen him before, shaking his mane (for it had apparently grown again) stood Aslan himself.

"Oh, Aslan!" cried both the children, staring up at him, almost as much frightened as they were glad....

"But what does it all mean?" asked Susan when they were somewhat calmer.

"It means," said Aslan, "that though the Witch knew the Deep Magic, there is a magic deeper still which she did not know. Her knowledge goes back only to the dawn of time. But if she could have looked a little further back, into the stillness and the darkness before Time dawned, she would have read there a different incantation. She would have known that when a willing victim who had committed no treachery was killed in a traitor's stead, the Table would crack and Death itself would start working backward."[2]

This clear and real display of both power and hope sustains the characters throughout the rest of the series of books. No matter how hard things become, they never despair like they did at the Stone Table. Now, they always have hope. There are times when they cannot see Aslan or experience his power, but they still remember how they witnessed these things at the Stone Table and it helps them have faith that they will see it again.

The analogy to Christ is, of course, intentionally very clear. Christ displayed His power to us when He walked on the earth and overcame death on the cross. Our challenge, living in the aftermath, is to believe this and walk in its truth—even when we can't see it or feel it—to allow the hope of His victory and His sacrifice to sustain us. God has not left us alone without examples and truths to anchor our hope. In this section we are going to be taking a look at how illustrated hope—hope found in stories and in the Bible and in God himself—will provide us with a sense of purpose that no experience in college or indeed in life can overcome.

Discussion / Reflection Questions

1. How does hope motivate and sustain us?

2. What does your hope rest on?

3. How does the hope of the Resurrection help guide us when life becomes challenging?

Chapter 10

Grounded Hope

Over and over in the lives of God's people, we see a pattern:
abundance alongside suffering, growing fruit but also dying seeds,
grace and the cross. Grace itself leads us to the world's broken places.

Andy Crouch, *Culture Making*

During my last two years at college, I tried to avoid morning classes—not because I didn't like them. I just found that living in a fraternity was not conducive to going to bed early, even if you wanted to. As a result, mornings became unappealing. During one semester, taking a class that started before eight was unavoidable. I accepted my fate and signed up. On the first morning, I was walking to class there was a heavy fog in the air, which made it difficult to see. I could hear footsteps ahead of me but for a while could not see anyone. As I drew closer, I realized the person in front of me was a fraternity member. However, this was not just any brother, it was one of the most popular guys in our house. The guy that everyone else wanted to emulate. A guy who was confident and funny and seemed to have his pick of friends or dates. But before I could say anything to him, he ducked out of the fog and into the counseling center. I was shocked. I could not believe that this guy—of all guys—would need help. In that moment it dawned on me that so often what we see of people is a façade, a show we put on for the world. We desperately want to make others believe we have it all together, so we hide the pain below the surface. No matter who we are, we all have a deep need for hope that cannot come from within ourselves.

The word hope is used more than 180 times in the Bible. It bookends the story of mankind in the Garden of Eden and in the New Heaven and the New Earth. God relentlessly steps in and provides hope to his followers again and again. In this chapter we're going to take a look at some of the most famous examples.

Adam and Eve

Adam and Eve are tempted by the crafty serpent. They give in and eat the forbidden fruit in the Garden of Eden. After they realize their folly, God brings down an intense sentence on them including pain in the birth of children for Eve and hard work for Adam. Yet even in this, God promises that a descendant of Eve will ultimately "bruise the head of the serpent."[1] This is the first prophecy referring to Christ's coming defeat of Satan on earth. In spite of the difficulties that Adam and Eve will encounter because of their sin, God provides a glimmer of restoration.

Abraham

In Genesis 12:1-3, God calls Abraham to leave everything that is comfortable and familiar:

> Now the LORD said to Abram, "Go forth from your country, and
> from your relatives and from your father's house, to the land which
> I will show you; and I will make you a great nation, and I will bless
> you, and make your name great; and so you shall be a blessing; and
> I will bless those who bless you, and the one who curses you I will
> curse. And in you all the families of the earth will be blessed."

God gives Abraham a bold call, one that will not be easy or seem efficient. Imagine taking your entire family and leaving the safety net you have always known to go somewhere you know nothing about. Today that may not seem as radical when we and lots of people we know have moved or lived thousands of miles away, but to Abraham this would have been a radical suggestion.[2] It was completely life-altering and countercultural. Abraham was a wealthy man (13:2), which in his day meant he had a lot of livestock. The effort required to pick up camp and move would have taken an inordinate amount of work and time, especially given that Abraham was seventy-five years old (12:4). Yet Abraham obeys God without question, "So Abram went forth as the Lord had spoken to him" (Genesis 12:4). There is no delay in his obedience or questioning of God's call. He simply trusts and obeys, because God provided him with a sense of hope and purpose. God promises to use this step to bless others for generations to come. He fulfills this promise as Abraham's lineage eventually led to Christ, through which all people have been blessed.

Joseph

Joseph's life is another one that was not without hardship. He was thrown into a pit by his brothers, taken as a slave to a foreign land where he knew no one, and then left in prison for years on end. How easy would it have been for Joseph to despair? Yet in all of this, God looks after him and uses these experiences to provide him with discernment beyond his years. During his time in Potiphar's house the Bible describes, "The Lord was with Joseph, so he became a successful man" (Genesis 39:2).[3] We see that Joseph recognizes God's hand of provision when he names his sons in Genesis 41: "Joseph named the firstborn Manasseh, 'For,' he said, 'God has made me forget all my trouble and all my father's household.' He named the second Ephraim, 'For,' he said, 'God has made me fruitful in the land of my affliction.'"

When Joseph is ultimately reunited with this family, we see one of the greatest stories of grace and forgiveness of all times. In an emotional scene, Joseph gives all the credit to God saying: "God sent me before you to preserve for you a remnant in the earth, and to keep you alive by a great deliverance. Now, therefore, it was not you who sent me here, but God; and He has made me a father to Pharaoh and lord of all his household and ruler over all the land of Egypt."[4]

Joseph kept his hope in God during all of those hard years. He also remained humble during the years of prosperity, clearly and boldly giving the credit to God instead of taking it for himself. Joseph realized that there was purpose in both times of trial and blessing.

Jeremiah

Jeremiah was a man who called an entire nation out of their sin. He stood apart and spoke boldly in a way that would not have been popular at all. To make his point clear, God had him create visual illustrations—like wearing an ox yoke around his neck when speaking against King Nebuchadnezzar to help people understand the consequences of their sin. God was going to allow the Israelites to be defeated by an enemy that would take them away from their homes and familiar places for multiple decades. It was a bleak picture and a sobering future. Yet in spite of the great consequences of their sin, God still provides a message of hope and restoration:

> For thus says the Lord, "When seventy years have been completed
> for Babylon, I will visit you and fulfill My good word to you, to bring
> you back to this place. For I know the plans that I have for you," de-
> clares the Lord, "plans for welfare and not for calamity to give you a
> future and a hope. Then you will call upon Me and come and pray to

Me, and I will listen to you. You will seek Me and find Me when you

search for Me with all your heart. I will be found by you," declares

the Lord, "and I will restore your fortunes and will gather you from

all the nations and from all the places where I have driven you,"

declares the Lord, "and I will bring you back to the place from where

I sent you into exile," (Jeremiah 29:10-14).

God promises to be found by the people. He realizes they need a time of separation, of living out the consequences of their own sin and folly, but He does not leave them there. He says that they can look forward to a time when they will be brought back to the land and experience a time of blessing. Even in one of the darkest periods of Israel's history, God provides a promise of hope. A vision they could cling to and look forward to during sleepless nights in an unknown and unfamiliar land.

Early Disciples

The disciples are charged with going and telling others about the story of Jesus who lived and walked among them. This was a relevant message because most of the early followers were Jews, burdened by the requirements of trying to earn God's favor by strictly obeying hundreds of rules. Over the years, the Jewish religious leaders had added to the law of God. They created a system of rules that few could remember and even fewer could actually follow.

The story of Cornelius is a wonderful example of the hope the early disciples brought. Cornelius is described as a devoted, God-fearing man. He is someone who is well-respected in his community, and yet something is missing. God orchestrates things in a miraculous way. He sends Peter to tell Cornelius about Christ—to offer the lasting hope that only He can provide. Peter is shocked and completely amazed that he is being asked to go outside of the Jewish nation to tell the Gentiles about Christ. Yet he faithfully obeys and as a result, Cornelius and his whole household receive the gift of the Holy Spirit, which is confirmation of his salvation and of Peter's calling to bring the gospel to the gentiles. There is great rejoicing that God did not leave Cornelius merely as a good person who did good works. He opened his eyes to the hope and power of the Holy Spirit and the story of Christ's redemptive work.

Revelation

Even on Judgment Day, hope is present. In the midst of great destruction and the unearthing of all of the world's sin, God tells us of a New Heaven and a New Earth. The things we see around us are not meant to last forever. He reveals that there will be no more darkness, sadness or night. In his ultimate and complete power, He will make all things new. He asks his believers to trust in this coming reality and draw strength from it today.

We could continue with examples of hope in the Bible, but the point is God has shown up in the past and He will do it again. God is for you. He created your innermost being and knows every day that has been ordained for you (Psalm 139). Let that truth wash over you. Stay in that reality. He is at work even in the hardest of circumstances to work things out for his glory and your good (Romans 8:28) and he wants you to believe that as you walk through college. Our ultimate end is not the shadow of this world, it is being united with him in heaven (Colossians 3:1-4).

Our church held a powerful service that further illustrates the way God redeems our stories for good. At the end of the service, a normal looking person appeared at the front with a hand-written note about a hardship or a sin in their own life. Then another person and another. The signs ranged from people battling intense illness to marriages that had gone south because of prioritizing work and material gain, to addiction, suicide of a family member and depression. There were about thirty people who literally paraded their transgressions and shortcomings before everyone. After an emotional and oppressive twenty minutes, the people began to turn their signs around revealing a second handwritten note: healed diseases, restored marriages, new hope and strength for today. It was a profound illustration of God at work in the lives right around us.

God will use the next four years to refine you, if you let him. He is not going to leave you, even if at times you may not feel a connection with him. So how do we take these truths about God and turn them into practical realities in our lives? That is what the rest of this book is about. We are going to look at how you can land in a place of encouragement in the midst of the struggles you are about to encounter over the next four years.

My hope is built on nothing less

Than Jesus' blood and righteousness;

I dare not trust the sweetest frame,

But wholly lean on Jesus' name.

On Christ, the solid Rock, I stand;

All other ground is sinking sand,

All other ground is sinking sand.

When He shall come with trumpet sound,

Oh, may I then in Him be found;

Dressed in His righteousness alone,

Faultless to stand before the throne.

On Christ, the solid Rock, I stand;

All other ground is sinking sand.[5]

Discussion / Reflection Questions

1. Do you know anyone who seems to have it all together on the outside but on the inside it's a different picture? Why do you think this is?

2. Which biblical character/story do you resonate with most? Why does that story provide you with hope and encouragement?

3. Sometimes what we know about God is difficult to put into practice in our lives. What are some practical ways that the promises of God impact your daily life?

Chapter 11

Believe in Christ

And you shall love the Lord your God with all your heart, and with
all your soul, and with all your mind, and with all your strength.

Mark 12:30

My business is blessed with the opportunity to assist elderly people by sending caregivers to help them in their homes. Many of our clients have lived incredible lives and had opportunities of privilege, power, and influence. When they find themselves in a position of needing a little extra assistance, it is often disconcerting and unsettling. A few years ago, I met one particular client who explained to me her caregiving needs. After going through the formalities of the assessment process, she looked directly at me and said, "David, I really want someone who can give me meaning and purpose in my life again. I am tired of just getting another year older." I was struck by her words and that she would look to us to meet this need. As I thought about it, I realized that the purpose and meaning she so desperately wanted could not be found in any caregiver—no matter how experienced they were. That kind of purpose is only available through Christ, and it is just as relevant at the end of life as it in when you head to college.

It all starts with a grounding belief in Christ. If you've gotten this far in this book, I'm guessing you probably have some kind of faith, but the thing about Jesus is that He is the Living God who is always calling us into a closer relationship with Him. We can always know Him better and love Him deeper, and that's what we're going to explore in this chapter.

First, we must acknowledge that we sin. This means we do things that do not please a perfect, holy God. If you have ever wondered if this is true, just spend some time with a two-year-old. Selfishness comes hard-wired. They see someone else playing with a toy and they decide they want it. They grab and cry until they get it. It is pretty fundamental, and yet it continues later in life with jobs, houses, and cars. Romans 3:23 says "for *all* have sinned and fall short of the glory of God."[1]

Basic human nature makes us think more highly of ourselves than we should, but God tells us that these bad things we do will lead to death (Romans 6:23). I love the way Max Lucado describes it in his book, *In the Grip of Grace.*

Suppose God simplified matters and reduced the Bible to one command: "Thou must jump so high in the air that you touch the moon." No need to love your neighbor or pray or follow Jesus; just touch the moon by virtue of a jump, and you'll be saved.

We'd never make it. There may be a few who jump three or four feet, even fewer who jump five or six; but compared to the distance we have to go, no one gets very far. Though you may jump six inches higher than I do, it's scarcely reason to boast.

Now God hasn't called us to touch the moon, but he might as well have. He said, "Therefore you are to be perfect, as your heavenly Father is perfect" (Matthew 5:48). None of us can meet God's standard. As a result, none of us deserves to don the robe and stand behind the bench and judge others. Why? We aren't good enough.

[Someone] may jump six inches, and you may jump six feet, but compared to the 230,000 miles that remain, who can boast? The thought of it is almost comical.[2]

Given that none of us are good enough to earn our way to heaven and that our sins deserve death, we have to believe Christ did it for us—that by coming down to earth and dying on the cross, he took our sins on himself and made life truly possible. "But God demonstrates His own love toward us, in that while we were yet sinners, Christ died for us," (Romans 5:8). John 3:16 also makes this truth very clear, "For God so loved the world that He gave His only begotten Son, that whoever believes in Him shall not perish, but have eternal life."

My father grew up in a church that preached about God giving you grace and freedom, but really had a lot of expectations for behavior. They expected you to be in church, go through the right steps in Sunday school, and be a very moral and upright person. When my dad got to college, he was worn out from trying to live out his faith on his own. It was there he first encountered the truth of what Jesus did for him on the cross. He understood the gospel for the first time and realized he needed to start from a place of belief and acceptance. From there, good works could flow out of him, not the other way around. It was transformational for him as he internalized Ephesians 2:8-9: "For by grace you have been saved through faith; and that not of yourselves, it is the gift of God; not as a result of works, so that no one may boast."

In your own faith journey, you need to get to that same place of humble acknowledgement and dependence on Christ. Live in the gratitude of what God has done for you and the freedom it provides.

Many well-intended believers miss the boat on God's abundant grace. Instead, they fall prey to a regimented series of lists and actions to keep themselves "on track" and right with God. Bryan Chapell describes this problem well in his book, *Holiness by Grace.*

> After initially trusting in Christ to make them right with God,
> many Christians embark on an endless pursuit of trying to satisfy
> God with good works that will keep him loving them. Such Chris-
> tians believe they are saved by God's grace but are kept in his care
> by their own goodness. This belief, whether articulated or buried
> deep in a psyche developed by the way we were treated by parents,
> spouses or others, makes the Christian life a perpetual race on a
> performance treadmill to keep winning God's affection ... While
> the Christian life can be characterized as a race, we persevere on
> the course God marks out for us not by straining to gain his affec-
> tion but by the assurance that he never stops viewing us from the
> perspective of his grace. God continually offers us unconditional
> love and the encouragement that our status as his children does
> not vary even though our efforts do.[3]

We must never lose sight of this as we seek to follow Christ. Deeds are a reflection and a natural outpouring of our faith, but never the source of it. You could follow the remaining advice in this book perfectly, but if you aren't trusting in Christ, it will leave you empty and unsatisfied.

Discussion / Reflection Questions

1. Sin is what keeps us from God. Confession opens the door to forgiveness. What are some sins in your life and how do they keep you from a closer relationship with God?

2. What is grace? How is Christ's death the ultimate display of God's grace?

3. In what ways do you try to earn God's love? If Christ died for our sins, why do we still try to earn God's love?

Chapter 12

Pursue the Father

A few years ago, our company's leadership team was debating whether to go into a new market. We evaluated a lot of different options and were a little daunted by the choices and the work required to get where we needed to be. We were stuck in the weeds. Losing sight of the big picture. Fortunately, we had an engaged consultant who, in a moment of clarity, stopped the conversation and said, "Guys, everything that is worth doing is hard. That's the opportunity in it. If it were easy everyone would be able to do it." We suddenly realized he was right and this propelled us to jump back in and engage with the problem and figure out this new market. With every new initiative since then, the wisdom of his words has become more apparent. Great ideas don't just happen. They are usually a by-product of someone coming up with the idea and then a lot of other people working behind the scenes to make it happen. Progress is made up not of one big leap, but rather of a hundred small steps along the way. To me, this is also a great picture of faith. It is one big decision, yes, but it's also a hundred small steps each and every day. Deep, rooted faith does not happen overnight.

That may sound like a lot of work, but it's really how all relationships work. Let me tell you another story to show what I mean.

When I first met my wife, Sarah, in college, I was blown away. I saw a depth to her character and was captivated by her beauty. I remember showing my little sister a picture of her and predicting that this would be the woman I would marry. I knew that if I could convince her to date me, I would be done—forever. But you know what? It took time—actually a lot of time. For years we were just friends. We ate dinner together each week and called this time our "friendship dinner." These meals happened with surprising regularity and often at obscure and (arguably) romantic restaurants. But if anyone got suspicious and asked Sarah whether there was anything going on between us, she would breezily tell them, "You don't need to worry about it at all. They are just friendship dinners." And she was right. I mean who could possibly be concerned with a friendship dinner? What could be more innocuous or harmless? But after about two years of these dinners, our relationship had progressed to the point of being very serious.

If I had started our relationship by telling Sarah I wanted to marry her, she would have refused me outright and likely never talked to me again. But after years of spending time together in a variety of settings, we realized that our relationship had gone well beyond friendship: spend enough time with someone and you will grow to love them in a deep and real way.

The same pattern is often true in our relationship with the Father. You will eventually come to a place of more fully understanding him after years of following Him. It is a process. Think about the people in your life who are the most spiritually mature. Chances are the first two people you thought of are older than you. They've had time to pursue Christ, to see Him work through a variety of situations in their lives and in those around them. They are equipped with a depth of wisdom and the ability to hear God's voice in a way that you, too, may know if you dedicate yourself to many years of pursuing God.

In his book about Paul, Chuck Swindoll makes the point that our own journey through circumstances allows us to comfort and relate to others who have those same circumstances. "Specific pain enables us to comfort others specifically."[1] When someone has been through cancer, they can relate to someone who has it in a way that you or I might not be able to. Abiding in Christ over an extended period of time and walking through life—seeking Him out in the situations and people you encounter—will develop a depth of spiritual life that simply cannot be obtained through shortcuts.

For a number of years, my family has been involved with a ministry called the CEO Forum. It was created by a guy called Mac McQuiston in order to provide support and encouragement to believers who lead companies. Mac once told me that whenever he starts coaching a new CEO, he always begins by working through a book called *Experiencing God*.[2] That's because Mac feels these leaders need a solid understanding of the basic tenets of walking in faith before they can move on to anything else.

One of the central points in *Experiencing God* is that you need to ask him to show you how he is at work in your life. God has things happening all around you that he wants you to be part of—if you're willing, that is. The author grounds this point in John 15:5: "I am the vine, you are the branches; he who abides in Me and I in him, he bears much fruit, for apart from Me you can do nothing." The metaphor is that Jesus is the vine and that from him, we live, and grow, and produce good things in our lives. When we try to do things on our own—or stop seeking him, our efforts will lead to futility and discouragement, just as grapes apart from the vine will only rot and die. Again, it takes time to understand this principle, but God is at work when you see circumstances align that you cannot explain in any way. Then you know you are on the right track. When you hear a sermon that "happens" to focus on something you just studied on your own that week, or when events in your life just happen to work out in a way you did not and could not have orchestrated, that's when you know you are abiding in Christ. He is inviting you into his work.

Practice Discipline

Jim Collins's business principles revolutionized many companies during their heyday. One of the central tenets in his teaching was that achieving goals and making progress in life requires three fundamental building blocks—disciplined thought, disciplined action and disciplined people.[3] These are powerful principles and ones that influenced me and my business. However, the origins of Jim's advice can probably be traced back to the Apostle Paul who encouraged us to live disciplined lives when he admonished us to "take every thought captive" (2 Corinthians 10:5) and again in Philippians 4:8: "Finally, brothers and sisters, whatever is true, whatever is worthy of respect, whatever is just, whatever is pure, whatever is lovely, whatever is commendable, if something is excellent or praiseworthy, think about these things" (NET). Our world and our actions all revolve around our "thought life."

Have you ever considered how our actions follow on from our thoughts? The first time I considered this idea at any length was during an English class when I was a freshman in college. It was one of those early spring days in Tennessee where the weather could not make up its mind if it wanted to be spring or summer. Moisture lingered in the air from the early morning showers but the sun was also out creating bright reflections in the puddles. The windows of every classroom were thrown open, and my class was led by a spirited English professor who was about five years older than us. She relished playing the antagonist in our class conversations because it challenged us to think deeper about the literature. That morning we were discussing a particular book in which the main character had made some poor choices in her life that originated from thoughts that had come to her mind. One of the girls in the class was insistent that the character's behavior was simply not her fault. She argued, "You cannot seriously blame this character for her thought life. There is no way to control what you think about—thoughts come as they please." The rest of the class seemed to generally agree. Only our professor stood on the other side of this debate. She pointed out that, even with a wandering thought life, the character certainly still had some responsibility for her actions.

When you care about something deeply, you think about it a lot and that often results in actions that help you obtain your goals. Your thoughts certainly influence your actions, and—depending on the thoughts—this can be a very useful thing. But thoughts don't result in action unless you're intentional about making them happen.

Ever since I was about thirteen, I'd dreamed of riding a bike from my house up to the lake where our family vacationed in Northern Indiana. On many occasions, I remember scheming about it with my buddies in spite of how crazy it sounded at that age. I kind of forgot about the dream until I turned thirty-five and realized I had better get on it if I was going to make it happen. But you know what? It was not enough just to think about the dream. It was not even enough to talk about the dream with friends. We had to actually take action: establish a training plan, block out the time on our calendars to do the rides, and then, of course, plan all the events around the actual day to make it happen. After about six months of training for the ride, God blessed us with a strong tailwind that helped push us the 130 miles needed to actually accomplish the goal. It ended up being a great time with some close buddies and I got to know a lot of rural roads in Indiana. But it would not have happened without the discipline required to plan and follow through and make my thoughts turn into actions.

"Incorporating discipline into your spiritual life can take on a lot of forms and can be daunting to think about especially during busy times in life, but at least three disciplines are worth thinking about related to your time in college—Solitude, Scripture and the Spirit."[4]

Preserve Solitude

The number of activities, clubs, social events, as well as the sheer volume of school work, will keep you very busy during the next few years of your life. It will require a constant balancing act to evaluate priorities and make decisions on which activities are the best use of your time. Believe it or not, this will help prepare you for life later on when demands on your time seem to never end. All of this will really challenge your ability to find solitude—even though solitude might perhaps be the most life-giving activity you could create for yourself in college. It will never seem urgent or important to do and there will always be something else vying for your attention.

In his book called *Playing God,* Andy Crouch has a section on the importance of solitude and Sabbath rest and what happens when we stop pursuing this: "a sabbathless life ends up with neither true work nor true rest, but with frantic and ineffective activity punctuated by couch-potato lethargy."[5] My wife found this to be true in college. She pushed herself to keep up with all of the activities and the demanding nature of her studies. After an exhausting few months in her sophomore year, her body told her it was time to stop when she was diagnosed with mono. It took her more than a month to rebound from the illness and caused her to rethink how she was approaching her college schedule.

Finding solitude requires discipline, and certainly Jesus is a model for us: "In the early morning, while it was still dark, Jesus got up, left the house, and went away to a secluded place, and was praying there" (Mark 1:35). Note that Jesus had to actually leave the house and go away to a place without distractions or interruptions to help him focus his heart and his mind on God. How often do we try to catch a few minutes to connect with God on the way out the door, or say a quick prayer before bed? My wife has modeled solitude for years in our house. She uses a specific chair in our family room when she is focusing her mind on God for the day. This particular chair is well positioned to afford an often glorious view of the sunrise. We all know that when Mom is sitting there, she is praying and connecting with God. I very rarely see her sitting in that chair later in the day, but the physical space helps her to focus and center herself for the day. Again, Andy Crouch describes it well: "For anyone who has succeeded in our always-on, noise-filled culture, an hour alone in a quiet room without the Internet, without recorded music and without a reassuring to-do list to accomplish is more than enough to reveal the true state of our hearts."[6] And therein lies the challenge—to make solitude a priority even when it does not seem productive or necessary. Henry Nouwen also challenges us to rethink when and where we can pursue solitude. It isn't as difficult as we think it is to make time for solitude: "It seems more important than ever to stress that solitude is one of the human capacities that can exist, be maintained and developed in the center of a big city, in the middle of a large crowd and in the context of a very active and productive life."[7] It is possible for you to develop a deep sense of connection with God and peace even in the midst of a busy campus—and essential that you do so.

Dig Deep

When you finally set aside time to connect with God, what do you do? God's primary method of revealing Himself to us today is through the Bible. It is amazing how much He will speak to you if you open your mind and your heart to His leading. David described it well when he said, "I have hidden your word in my heart that I might not sin against you" (Psalm 119:11, NIV). In Hebrews, the centrality and power of God's written word are emphasized clearly, "For the Word of God is living and active and sharper than any two-edged sword, and piercing as far as the division of soul and spirit, of both joints and marrow, and able to judge the thoughts and intentions of the heart" (Hebrews 4:12).

Delivering *Your* Future

We have to seek out wisdom from God instead of just being influenced by the culture of the day and the other pressures that will come at us. But how should we study the Word? At Dallas Seminary, we took a whole class on this topic, and it boils down to three straightforward steps:

1. Observation

What is the context of the passage you read: what comes immediately before and after it? What did you notice about the verses? What is the text literally saying?

2. Interpretation

What does the observation mean? What is the author trying to say?

3. Application

How can you apply the truth today or relate it to your life?

Let's look at an example using a passage from James.

"But if any of you lacks wisdom, let him ask of God, who gives to all generously and without reproach, and it will be given to him. But he must ask in faith without any doubting, for the one who doubts is like the surf of the sea, driven and tossed by the wind. For that man ought not to expect that he will receive anything from the Lord, being a double-minded man, unstable in all his ways" (James 1:5-8).

1. Observation—If I lack wisdom about something, I should ask God.

2. Interpretation—I am not expected to be all-wise. God wants me to come to him.

3. *Application*—I should identify a specific situation today that I need help with, and ask God to give me wisdom.

This is a simple way to jump into any passage. It will help you direct your thoughts and reflections about the verses you're reading.

Discussion / Reflection Questions

1. How is God at work in your life? If you're not sure, ask Him to show you.

2. Thoughts influence our actions, so what is it that you spend time thinking about? How often do your thoughts return to God?

3. How does our pursuit of solitude affect our relationship with God?

Chapter 13

Seek Out the Spirit

When we try to follow Jesus without being filled daily with the Spirit, we
find ourselves frustrated by our failures and exhausted by our efforts.

Kyle Idleman, *Not a Fan*

Many Christians pursue a formulaic approach to faith that can become monotonous and devoid of emotion. You can have an amazing quiet time every day, but if you do not allow room for the Holy Spirit to work in your life, you will miss out on some of the most dynamic and exciting ways God wants to use you. So how do you really live by the Spirit?

Even the best and brightest theologians have struggled to simplify the Spirit of God into a set of principles or a concise analogy. He is beyond our understanding, and yet when Christ told the disciples about the Spirit and the power he would bring, he used no uncertain terms, "but you will receive power when the Holy Spirit has come upon you; and you shall be My witnesses" (Acts 1:8). Let's look at two of the most helpful texts about the Spirit to learn more:

> And Christ lives within you, so even though your body will die because of sin, the Spirit gives you life because you have been made

right with God. The Spirit of God, who raised Jesus from the dead, lives in you. And just as God raised Christ Jesus from the dead, He will give life to your mortal bodies by this same Spirit living within you.

Therefore, dear brothers and sisters, you have no obligation to do what your sinful nature urges you to do. For if you live by its dictates, you will die. But if through the power of the Spirit you put to death the deeds of your sinful nature, you will live. For all who are led by the Spirit of God are children of God.

So you have not received a spirit that makes you fearful slaves. Instead, you received God's Spirit when he adopted you as his own children. Now we call him, "Abba, Father." For his Spirit joins with our spirit to affirm that we are God's children. And since we are his children, we are his heirs. In fact, together with Christ we are heirs of God's glory. But if we are to share his glory, we must also share his suffering (Romans 8:10-17, NLT).

From this text we can know that God lives in us through the Spirit. That he not only provides us with help in struggles with our natural sinful desires, but the Spirit also provides us with real life on this earth. Through his work in our lives we can also know that we are children of God. Let's take a look at the second text from John.

Nicodemus said to Him, "How can a man be born when he is old? He cannot enter a second time into his mother's womb and be born, can he?" Jesus answered, "Truly, truly, I say to you, unless one is born of water and the Spirit he cannot enter into the kingdom of God. "That which is born of the flesh is flesh, and that which is born of the Spirit is spirit. "Do not be amazed that I said to you, 'You must be born again.' The wind blows where it wishes and you hear the sound of it, but do not know where it comes from and where it is going; so is everyone who is born of the Spirit" (John 3:4–8).

From this text we learn from Jesus that the presence of the Spirit in our lives is what allows us to "enter the kingdom of God." This is a promise of heaven and life after death guaranteed by the Spirit. By the Spirit we also receive our day-to-day instruction from the Lord. It is the Spirit who also gives us our identity in Christ; as being born automatically gives you identity as part of a human family, so being born of the Spirit gives you identity in Christ and makes you a child of God's family.

Both of these texts are rich in how they articulate who the Spirit is and how he works in our lives. Below is a summary of some of the things mentioned above as well as some other things that the Bible says the Spirit does in the lives of believers:

- Helps you in struggles

- Provides your identity in Christ

- Reminds you of God's truth

- Lives inside of you

- Provides real life on this earth

- Keeps your spirit alive after you die

- Empowers you to turn from sin

- Calls you a child of God

- Orchestrates events in your life to bring about transformation

- Directs and leads you in the day-to-day

One of the most compelling ways to connect more with the Holy Spirit is to notice how God is trying to get your attention through experiences and encounters in your life. In his second memoir, titled *Now and Then*, Frederick Buechner expresses that "listening to your life" is the true essence and legacy of his writings:

> If I were called upon to state in a few words the essence of every-
> thing I was trying to say both as a novelist and as a preacher it would
> be something like this: Listen to your life. See it for the fathomless
> mystery that it is. In the boredom and pain of it no less than in the
> excitement and gladness: touch, taste, smell your way to the holy
> and hidden heart of it because in the last analysis all moments are
> key moments, and life itself is grace.[1]

God is trying to get your attention and it is often through the work of the Spirit in your life. There are at least three principles that I have found to be important in learning to walk in the Spirit.

Watch for Hinge Events

One of my life mentors is a successful man who has managed to keep life in perspective both for himself and his family. He's a deep soul whom I enjoy being around but who also makes me a little uncomfortable because I'm never sure what he'll say next. He asks direct questions that penetrate superficiality. In one of our discussions, he explained the concept of hinge events— critical junctures in your life that God brings about to move you to the next point. Sometimes you don't even realize they're happening. They literally serve as a hinge to take you from one place in your life to the next. It could be a simple conversation with a friend that leads to a connection with another friend who plays a critical role in your life for years to come. Or someone else that connects you with an opportunity in your profession you didn't know existed before. These "hinge events" most often happen as a result of people either being led by the Spirit to work in your life or as a result of your responding to the Spirit in your own life.

After college, a good friend was insistent on introducing us to another couple who she thought we would really like. I wasn't sure, but something told me I should just give it a try. I'm so glad I listened to this prompting because it turned out to be a hinge event in our lives. What seemed like a causal connection has turned into long-term and very intentional relationship with the couple. Our families have influenced each other in countless ways over the years ranging from navigating sports with young kids, to disciplining our kids, to engaging with others in our lives, to trusting in God to provide resources for our daily needs. We would have never known this family without that friend taking that initial step—listening to the Spirit's leading in her own life created a hinge event for us that transformed our lives.

Pay Attention to Emotions

Emotions are tricky because, at times, they can mislead you when you listen to them in isolation, or rather without a community around you or the Bible to act as a guide. However, God gave us our emotions and they can often be the window into a deeper part of life. Fredrick Buechner's words again help us to understand this concept:

> You never know what may cause them. The sight of the Atlantic Ocean can do it, or a piece of music, or a face you've never seen before. A pair of somebody's old shoes can do it.... You can never be sure. But of this you can be sure. Whenever you find tears in your eyes, especially unexpected tears, it is well to pay the closest attention. They are not only telling you something about the secret of who you are, but more often than not God is speaking to you through them of the mystery of where you have come from and is summoning you to where, if your soul is to be saved, you should go next.[2]

Emotions are not efficient. As Buechner describes, they "well up" from unexpected places. The positive ones never seem to last quite long enough in the theater of our minds. Paying attention to these wellsprings of life, the inner way of the leading, is vital to staying connected with the Spirit. They are glimpses into the full and utter joy we will experience when we are finally united with God—fully known and fully loved.

A few weekends ago, I was going through some old boxes from college and came across the first handwritten letter I wrote to my wife. That was back when we used to use paper and pens occasionally. In this letter, I poured out my heart to my future wife for one of the first times in a vulnerable and authentic way. A wash of joy came over me as I remembered the exact place I wrote the letter, how anxious I was to send it and how hopeful I was that it would be well-received. Sarah and I had a sweet moment of connection as a result and I was glad I took the time to feel the memory.

Negative emotions are even more challenging and inconvenient. In his TV program for children, Mr. Rogers encouraged his audience to face the hard emotions – to get to the root of the things that feel fearful or uncertain:

> Anything that's human is mentionable, and anything that is mentionable can be more manageable. When we can talk about our feelings, they become less overwhelming, less upsetting, and less scary. The people we trust with that important talk can help us know that we are not alone.[3]

After Fred Rogers passed away, Tim Madigan wrote about his lifelong friendship with him. Tim describes how Fred encouraged him to enter into the sadness, to talk about the memories behind the emotions. How in spite of Fred's demanding schedule, he always made time for him and helped him feel like he was one of the most important people in the world. He gave Tim the time and space to process his emotions instead of discounting them as unimportant.

Tim describes how it was challenging to allow himself to feel his emotions during the conversations with Fred and how listening to certain songs seemed to help him connect more with the inner way of his heart. They allowed him to feel God's presence more fully, to slow down and to become more aware of God's leading in his life. A few months after my dad passed away rather abruptly, we were driving home from a park where the boys had been riding and running well into the night. They had sensed adventure and the thrill of being out later than usual with a rowdy group of boys. Cold-play's song "Daddy" came on and it immediately washed over us with very real sense of sadness and loss as we realized how "far away" Dad was from us now and how he would no longer be able "to come out and stay." One of my sons was particularly close to my dad and I will never forget how he clung to me as we embraced while the song was ending—finally releasing some of sadness and loss that was lurking below the sur-face. However, without the song and an acceptance of emotions, we would have most certainly missed out on something very beautiful.

The challenge is that God has given us our emotions—both the ones we enjoy feeling and those we don't so much—to help us connect with deeper streams in our life. If you stop living out of your heart, then eventually you start missing out on God working in your life and in the lives of those around you. The Pixar movie *Inside Out* portrays this truth well. The movie is set inside the mind of a young girl and each of the main characters are one of her emotions. The anger character lives in a state of constant frustration and is incessantly ready to stir things up. The sad character is melodramatic and self-absorbed, and as a result is often pushed aside by the other characters. The effervescent joy character seems to be the one who always helps all the other emotions pull together and win the day. However, in the end, the story shows us that the only way to walk through challenges and solve real problems with authenticity and integrity is to pull from each emotion—even sadness. We need all of our emotions to work in concert with each other. As Solomon tells us, "For everything there is a season, and a time for every purpose under heaven … a time to weep, and a time to laugh; a time to mourn, and a time to dance" (Ecclesiastes 3:1, 4, NKJV).

Recently, I planned a weekend to talk with my sons about the teenage years they were about to enter into. It had been a frantic week at work, but I woke up very early on Saturday and felt the need to prepare for our time together. As the morning progressed, we worked through some tough material that led to real transparency. We talked about what it means to become a man—the very real challenge of going through adolescence, the new sexual temptations they would face and the stronger emotions they would feel. My two older boys expressed sadness, encouragement and admonition in a string of very real emotions. I found myself weeping alongside of them as they shared their vulnerable hearts with each other and with me. I reflected on how I desired for God to be preeminent in their lives. It was a breakthrough, both for my relationship with my boys and for their relationship with each other. The emotions seemed to lead us there and allow us to transcend to new levels of closeness that we couldn't have otherwise.

Obey in the First Fifteen Seconds

One of the most interesting aspects of the Spirit is that when he leads in your life, he does not force obedience. He often directs you down a path that might be more beneficial than another but he does not require it. A retired surgeon, who was influential in my community, once admonished a group of younger men to obey God's prompt within the first fifteen seconds. If we don't, we are prone to distraction and may forget to act. In his Book, *Love Does*, Bob Goff encourages the same idea by motivating us to take action. Love doesn't just sit around and think about doing something—it takes action. Loving God means taking action when we hear His voice.

A few years back, a couple in full-time ministry at our church fell on some financially tough times. The final straw came when their car broke down. Repairing the car wasn't an option, but neither did they have the money to buy a new one. The wife dreamed of having a brand new Honda minivan, even though she knew they could never afford it. They were out of options—that is until something amazing happened. The same day their car broke down, word got out among the congregation at our church. Someone felt the Spirit's call and they responded immediately. That night, the couple received an anonymous phone call from a Honda dealership informing them that a large sum of money had been given for them to go to the Honda dealership and pick out a new minivan. It was a moment of euphoria for the family and a clear reminder that God was still at work in their lives.

Delivering *Your* Future

Pretty cool story, right? Except that's not where it ends.

A few months later, the wife's Lyme disease became more pronounced. Then she was diagnosed with an aggressive cancer. Once again, the world felt like it was crumbling around her: her body ached, the kids were fighting, and the house seemed to never get cleaned up. But in those moments of pain and doubt, she began going to the garage, getting in her minivan and closing her eyes. She would breathe in the new-car smell and remind herself of God's abundant provision in her life. Sitting there with her eyes closed she would tell herself that God was still active in her life and that he would not leave her no matter how hard things got. What started as a kind gift led by the Spirit's prompting, God then used as a symbol of His faithfulness to this woman—something much more valuable to her in the end than a new car.

Brennan Manning describes it well when he says, "Each moment of our existence, we are either growing into more or retreating into less. We are either living a little more or dying a little bit."[4] The Spirit is calling you to live a little more by obeying him, to step into deeper water. He wants you to get out of the boat like Peter did in the storm. Peter lost his footing when he looked at the tumultuous water around him, but when he shifted his gaze to Christ's all-knowing eyes, he could walk on the water.

Watch for the ways God shows up through people and circumstances in your life, and pay attention to "hinge" events that seem to move you from one point to the next. Lean into emotions, even if they are hard and awkward, and obey the Spirit's leading quickly and radically. The radical blessing of the Spirit is that he is with us every moment—he cares for you and loves you infinitely.

Discussion / Reflection Questions

1. How has listening to the Spirit led to hinge events in your life?

2. How does the Spirit speak to us through our feelings? Can you recall a time when you obeyed his voice and it led to something unexpected?

3. Do you act right away when you hear the voice of the Spirit or do you sometimes delay? Why?

Chapter 14

Making Hope Practical

Hope is the most powerful force in the universe. With hope you

can inspire nations to greatness. With hope you can raise up the

downtrodden. With hope you can ease the pain of unbearable loss.

William McRaven, *Make Your Bed*

The road to healing takes a while sometimes. After wanting to end my life, I grappled with how far my sin and despair could take me. I wanted to get away and reflect, so I went on a retreat to the desolate Upper Peninsula of Michigan. Of course, my parents were nervous about me going. I can't blame them—especially since, for a moment, my mother thought her son's life had ended on that gloomy night in southern Indiana. But the leader of the retreat assured them I would be in a safe place. Plus, my friend who had accompanied me to the ER was planning to go on the trip as well.

The drive took about ten hours and seemed never-ending. I had no idea how far north Michigan goes nor how truly remote it gets. When we passed the final bridge and neared the camp, I began to sense renewal and purpose I had not felt in a long time. It was as if God was telling me that it would be okay. His grace was sufficient for me and His power is made perfect in weakness.

The week was filled with meaningful connections with other believers and an opportunity to experience God through the rawness of nature. I am convinced that when you go that far north, you see some of the biggest displays of God's glory. The stars are remarkably clear and seem to go on forever. The water is clean and seems untouched as on the day of Creation. I don't remember all of the theology we studied, but I remember laughing a lot and feeling a sense of wholeness again. It was the start of a journey that eventually helped me to understand how to walk daily in the grace and power the Holy Spirit offers believers.

But this transformation did not happen overnight. The retreat set me on a course to start reorienting my perspective on life. To know myself, accept myself and be myself.[1] It has taken years and I still do not have it all down, but the principles that follow are what helped to shape my worldview and propel me into the next stage of life. I had to believe that God was for me and had a plan. Then I had to be patient and faithful in the process. I had to turn from the siren's song of our culture that demands immediate gratification and instant fixes.

The next section of this book is going to be more practical in nature with the caveat that I believe God is a God of clarity and order. He loves it when His children really grasp His truths in a way that is tangible and real. As a result, the guidelines that follow are organized and somewhat linear in their delivery, but I do not want them to be taken as a set of legalistic rules or a formula that when followed will lead to "success" in college. Think of them more as signposts along the way. Being aware of them and applying them will help to illuminate your path and provide you with a right orientation.

Discussion / Reflection Questions

1. Have you ever found yourself someplace where the beauty of creation reveals something of God's glory to you? What did it feel like?

2. Is there anything in your life that needs God's healing?

3. Have you ever asked Him to begin healing your heart and mind and to fill you with His Spirit? If not, why not do that now?

PART III: PRACTICAL HOPE

Chapter 15

Create Balance

All extremes except extreme devotion to [God] are to be encouraged.

C. S. Lewis, *The Screwtape Letters*

Think about the changes in environment and life-pattern you're about to experience. In high school, you made some choices about your schedule and your patterns of behavior, but most things were pretty well established for you. You knew what time school started, the periods and the class schedules. The school day was clearly mapped out with multiple, loud bells to remind you in case you got distracted. Then there was the slew of extracurricular activities that kept you going well into the night to boost your resume and prepare you for the college experience. Add some homework to the mix and you likely had very full days. In college, all of that changes. You get to pick when you want to be in class, and you'll have a lot more free time to fill in between. Your parents are not there to tell you what do and how to make choices along the way. Most young adults who hit college are ready for that level of freedom, but if they are honest, they also admit that it can result in misplaced priorities at times. Danish philosopher Søren Kierkegaard said that, "human beings were made to love God supremely, center their lives on him above anything else, and build their very identities on him. Anything other than this is sin."[1] Therefore, the problem with sin is not just doing bad things, but the making of good things into ultimate things. As Pastor Mark Vroegop says, we take good things and make them into god things.[2] One of the most effective ways to avoid these extremes is to create a balance.

When I was in college, I developed debilitating migraine headaches. They would rock my world and usually began with losing my peripheral vision in both eyes, followed by violent nausea, slurred speech and then a massive headache that lasted for hours. I went to a slew of doctors to try to get help with the symptoms. During one migraine, I made the unfortunate choice to drive. Because I could not see anything on either side of me, I hit a landscaping trailer that propelled the left side of my jeep into the air. When I became aware of my surroundings again, I realized I was upside down in the car, still buckled in. The jeep had landed upside down with the wheels spinning in the air. As I crawled out of the window through the broken glass, I remember thanking God I was even alive and able to get out. A brush with death has a way of sharpening our thinking, and as I looked back on the times these headaches would occur, a few patterns emerged. They would almost always happen during a season of high stress when I was usually compromising my balance significantly by cutting sleep, not hydrating enough, eating haphazardly and often not connecting with others in a way that would allow me to normalize the pressure I was feeling. The migraines did not really stop until after I got out of college and my wife helped me develop more rhythm in my life. Instead of pushing every aspect of my life to the extreme in a constant effort to maximize productivity, she encouraged me to develop discipline in rest, rejuvenation and "soul care". As a result of her encouragement and my commitment to changing, over time, my migraines have largely dissipated.

Regardless of how the problem manifests itself in your life, understanding balance will be really important over the next few years, and it will not come naturally. Dr. Keith Douds is the Director of Alliance Psychology Group in Long Beach, California. He describes it as finding a cadence or a rhythm to life, creating a sense of routine and structure that allows you to take care of your physical body in addition to your spirit.

A few boundaries or guidelines will go a long way. One of them is how much sleep you need. Many people in college skirt the edges on sleep. They are prone to staying up way too late, and after a while they are so exhausted that they often get sick or have a nervous breakdown. Thinking through how much sleep you realistically need to function effectively and then scheduling your classes to allow you to get that sleep will be important. My wife was a master at all this. Throughout college, she would sign up for classes at 8:00 a.m. to make sure she was up and going. This also made her go to bed at a reasonable hour because if she did not, she would be exhausted after a few days.

Another boundary you can create is determining your priorities and then managing your time to accomplish them. Many students coming into college may not have worked very hard in high school. The difficulty of the workload as well as the accompanying freedom of the schedule may surprise them. It's human nature to procrastinate, and this is never more easy to do than in college. Take time to look at your calendar and block out when you will prepare for your classes, how you will get your workouts in and when you will have time with friends. If you don't, it's likely that these things won't happen. I love the analogy of a chef. You would never expect a chef to walk into a kitchen and start cooking meals for fifty people without any preparation. Instead, the chef has to carefully plan out the menu in advance, order the necessary ingredients and make sure the team is in place to serve patrons. When all of that happens, patrons enjoy wonderful culinary experiences. In the same way, you need to block out some time each week to wrap up the last week and plan for the next week. If you do not, requests that "come along" will take over your time.

In Stephen Covey's book *The Seven Habits of Highly Effective People*, he talks about the concept of getting the big rocks in first.[3] In a classic illustration in his seminars, he provides a selection of rocks—all shapes and sizes—to a woman and asks her to fit them into a jar. He says the rocks represent important things in our lives like family, school, volunteering and fitness. He also provides her with a bucket of sand. The sand represents all the little things that come up in life and vie for our attention. Unwittingly, the woman starts by putting the sand (the little things) into the jar first and then tries to cram in the large rocks. After trying for some time, she becomes frustrated and has to leave out really important rocks like personal health and big projects she needs to work on. Dr. Covey then suggests that she start by putting the big rocks in first. When she does this, she is able to pour the sand over the top and it all fits in the jar. By placing the big rocks in first, she keeps her priorities and gets most of the little things accomplished as well.

The same will be true for you in college: you need to decide what the big rocks are for the week and make sure that they have a place in your schedule. When you do this, you will be surprised at how many of the little things you complete as well. Start your week by asking yourself, what are the top three things that must happen this week? If I get nothing else accomplished this week, what three things do I need to get done?

An important aspect of taking care of yourself is also allowing for rest. Genesis 2:2 says, "By the seventh day God completed His work which He had done, and He rested on the seventh day from all His work which He had done." If the Creator of the world thought it was important enough to rest, why do we get too busy to take a break and disconnect from the pressures?

The first semester of business schools is often the hardest semester and can put a lot of pressure on students. After a grueling few months of studies and group work, I remember feeling stressed and tired. After finally finishing my last exam, I was walking through the wood-paneled halls of the Tuck School of Business while the snow swirled outside. The classrooms were quiet as many students had already left. As I passed by one of the dean's offices, I stepped in to thank her for her help with the semester. She responded by encouraging me to enjoy a "well-deserved" break.

As I stepped out into the world blanketed with snow, I remember thinking how ironic it was that the dean had to affirm my taking a break. I realized that when left to myself, I am prone to continue to toil under the weight of the constant pressure I put on myself instead of embracing Christ as he encouraged, "Come to me, all you who are weary and burdened, and I will give you rest. Take my yoke on you and learn from me, because I am gentle and humble in heart, and you will find rest for your souls" (Matthew 11:28-30, NET).

Part of creating balance is practicing a Sabbath or taking time off from your work and school. I had a few friends in college who were disciplined about not doing work on Sundays. It seemed crazy to me to attempt it given the workload, but they pulled it off. Looking back, they were some of the most centered people, and certainly seemed to be less swayed by the turmoil and inner anxiety the rest of us constantly endured. Even if your "Sabbath" is not a deeply spiritual day—perhaps time spent with friends or pursuing hobbies, it will still help to re-orient you for the week ahead. There is also no need to be rigid about it—if you can get half a day or even a few hours it will make a difference.

Discussion / Reflection Questions

1. When in your life have you felt unbalanced by too much activity? What factors drove you to this point?

2. When have you been the most balanced? Are there activities or ways you spent your time that helped you contribute to balance?

3. What is one thing you can do this week to seek out balance and rhythm?

Chapter 16

Lock Arms

All for One and One for All.

Alexandre Dumas, *The Three Musketeers*

The fabled Three Musketeers were part of the French army between 1789 and 1816, and it was the novels by Alexandre Dumas that made their stories legendary. Dumas' masterful epic is full of political intrigue, action-adventure and dynamic characters. There are three original Musketeers—Athos, Porthos and Aramis—who are later joined by the brash, young D'Artagnan, who has a knack for getting in over his head.

Each Musketeer has unique strengths and, throughout their adventures, they shift roles and complement each other. Porthos is a giant among men: someone with uncharacteristic strength who heroically helps the Musketeers out of many tight situations. He does not always think through the whole situation, but instead rushes in with strength, enthusiasm and fortitude. Aramis is intelligent, calculating and at times manipulative. Athos is noble, loyal and protective, although he is prone to deep regret. The plot is driven by their collective strengths and shortcomings, but their devotion to each other and their cause is unwavering.

God tells us that people have been made in His image, which means that as His followers, we each reflect God in a different way. Thus, our picture of God is incomplete without getting to know others He has created and by inviting them to share in our own story. But by inviting them to share in our story we also begin to share in their story until the difference between the two becomes indistinguishable. One of the most poignant scenes in all *The Three Musketeers* books comes after a particularly tense battle. Porthos has overcome insurmountable obstacles to help his friends and their cause, but at last finds himself trapped after an explosion topples rubble onto him:

"Porthos! Porthos!" cried Aramis, tearing his hair. "Porthos! where are you? Speak!"

"There, there!" murmured Porthos, with a voice growing evidently weaker; "patience! patience!" Scarcely had he pronounced these words, when the impulse of the fall augmented the weight; the enormous rock sank down, pressed by the two others which sank in from the sides, and, as it were, swallowed up Porthos in a sepulcher of broken stones. On hearing the dying voice of his friend... Aramis, animated, active, and young as at twenty, sprang toward the triple mass, and with his hands, delicate as those of a woman, raised by a miracle of vigor a corner of the immense sepulcher of granite. Then he caught a glimpse, in the darkness of that grave, of the still brilliant eye of his friend, to whom the momentary lifting of the mass restored a moment of respiration. The two men came rushing up, grasped their iron levers, united their triple strength, not merely to raise it, but to sustain it. All was useless. The three men slowly gave way with cries of grief, and the rough voice of Porthos, seeing them exhaust themselves in a useless struggle, murmured in a bantering tone those last words which came to his lips with the last breath, "Too heavy!"

After which the eye darkened and closed, the face became pale, the hand whitened, and the Titan sank quite down, breathing his last sigh. With him sank the rock, which even in his agony he had still held up. The three men dropped the levers, which rolled upon the tumulary stone. Then, breathless, pale, his brow covered with sweat, Aramis listened, his breast oppressed, his heart ready to break.

Nothing more! The giant slept the eternal sleep, in the sepulcher which God had made to his measure.

Aramis, silent, icy, trembling like a timid child, arose shivering from the stone. A Christian does not walk upon tombs. But though capable of standing, he was not capable of walking. It might be said that something of Porthos, dead, had just died within him.[1]

When Porthos dies, part of Aramis dies with him. That is true of our close friends too; we feel a deep sense of loss when they are no longer part of our lives—so deep that it feels as though we have lost something of us as well as losing them. One of my close friends recently lost his wife. In the months that followed her passing, he realized they had grown together in ways he had not even realized during their twenty years of being together. He said it felt like part of him was no longer here—no one was there to finish his sentences or help him think through the deeper issues of parenting and life.

Friends often believe more in you than you do yourself; they see the ways Christ is reflected in you more than you do yourself. They help you see the good in you and to realize the ways God has gifted you even when you cannot. I love this description from Dr. John Hannah: "Friends don't believe the best things about you because they know you are a liar. They also don't believe the worst things about you because they know you are a liar."[2]

John Eldredge has written a lot about our need for friendship, especially with men. He calls it a "band of brothers." A group of guys that will come alongside you, lock arms with you and help you walk through life.[3] People who you can be honest and vulnerable with while also sharing adventures together. Women are much more naturally gifted at this than men. God has created women to be comfortable with sharing emotions and connecting quickly with others. Women are able to bring quick discernment and insight into their relationships. However even with their superior relational abilities, women in college can get caught up in the rush to know everyone or socially climb over developing authentic relationships. In this chapter, we're going to examine three aspects of locking arms: realizing God's intent with community, aligning with others, and recognizing glimpses of God in each other.

Realizing God's Intent with Community

Any earnest reflection of God will quickly lead you to realize that God's very nature is about community. He intends for us to live in community, and he models it. The three persons of God - Father, Son and Holy Spirit - are perhaps the best representation we have of unity with differentiation. The trinity relationship kicks off the first story in the Bible. God, the Father, creates the world and walks with Adam and Eve. We learn from John that Christ (the Word) took an active part as well: "In the beginning was the Word, and the Word was with God, and the Word was God. He was in the beginning with God. All things came into being through Him, and apart from Him nothing came into being that has come into being. In Him was life, and the life was the Light of men" (John 1:1-4).

The Father and the Son were working in tandem to create life as we know it. Their perfect, integrated relationship resulted in the awe of snow-capped mountain ranges touching the clouds and the beauty of the sun creeping over the horizon of the open ocean to start the day. They used their creative genius to make man in their image with unique personalities and giftings.

The Spirit was also a part of creation. "The earth was formless and void, and darkness was over the surface of the deep, and the Spirit of God was moving over the surface of the waters" (Genesis 1:2). In the opening act of this incredible narrative, God is acting in concert: in community. The three persons of God are working together to create beauty, life and depth in the world.

Millennia later, Jesus takes on flesh and walks among us as fully God and fully man. Yet, He often leaves in the early morning to spend time with His Father. On the night He is going to be betrayed He implores His disciples to remain watchful and pray to His Father. In perhaps the most dramatic moment of the whole Bible, the Father turns his back on His beloved son: "Jesus cried out with a loud voice, saying ... 'my God, my God, Why have you forsaken me?'" (Matthew 27:46). To be disconnected from His Father rips apart the very core of who Jesus is—shattering the community and fellowship they have enjoyed since the beginning of time.

When Christ returns from the dead, He sends the Spirit to help the believers. Throughout Acts and the New Testament, we see the third member of the Trinity emerge.

Cleary, we cannot anticipate that our relationships and community will be as close as the Trinity. After all, they are of the same essence—the Godhead—but it is significant that God chooses to reveal Himself to us in the three persons of the trinity and emphasizes to us how important relationships are to God.

Delivering *Your* Future

Outside of the Trinity, the Bible has many stories of community. The second commandment admonishes us to love our neighbors as ourselves. We learn in Galatians 5:14 that "the entire law is fulfilled in keeping this one command: 'Love your neighbor as yourself'" (NIV). We are called to love God first and then love those around us.

The story of Jonathan and David is a great story of friendship, sacrifice and mutual respect. The Bible says that Jonathan loved David "as he loved his own life" (1 Samuel 20:17). Jonathan believes that David is called to take over his father's throne and actively helps him escape King Saul's plans to destroy him. Their friendship gave each other strength and allowed them to see God reflected in each other.

The story of Ruth and Naomi may also be one of the greatest friendships in the Bible. Ruth knowingly leaves her home to follow and support Naomi after Ruth's husband dies. She selflessly lays aside her own comforts to help Naomi re-establish herself. Naomi in turn encourages Ruth to pursue Boaz. She believes in her daughter-in-law in a way that results in an incredible transformation in both of their lives.

While Christ walked the earth, he intentionally spent time with the same group of guys—the twelve disciples—and made it very clear that they were supposed to minister together. As C. S. Lewis says, "first of all, Jesus sends the twelve out in pairs (Mark 6:7). We keep forgetting that we are being sent out two-by-two. We cannot bring the good news on our own. We are called to proclaim the gospel together in the community."[4] Like the early disciples, God wants us to minister and lead with others engaged with us. We aren't called to do it all on our own. Recently, I was meeting with my friend Tim. Tim is a highly-talented leader who wants to love God with his whole heart, serve his wife well and develop meaningful community. By all outward (and most inward) measures, Tim is succeeding. Part of Tim's ministry has been to lead a small group at our church. As we talked about his leadership with the group, Tim expressed feelings of burnout. For four years he had found the content, led the discussion, coordinated the logistics, and now, with a second small child on the way, it was becoming too much.

When I suggested that he divide up the work and invite others to join with him in the responsibilities of leadership and facilitation, I could literally see the weight lift off his shoulders. The others who were in the group were more than happy to step up and share the load. Tim needed to hear that he did not need to do it all on his own. We all need to hear that sometimes.

The disciples were never meant to do it on their own and neither are you—especially in college. Pastor Timothy Keller puts it this way: "Christians commonly say they want a relationship with Jesus, that they want to 'get to know Jesus better.' You will never be able to do that by yourself. You must be deeply involved in the church, in Christian community, with strong relationships of love and accountability. Only if you are part of a community of believers seeking to resemble, serve and love Jesus will you ever get to know Him and grow into His likeness."[5] Keller's words get at the heart of the idea of community. If you embrace the notion that God, at his core, is a God of community, then we should be a people of community. You need to align with other believers. Seek out people who can deeply encourage you to follow God and who are not afraid to call you out when you lose your way and build you up when they see the glory God has given you.

Aligning with Others

When you arrive at college, you leave the support system of your family, friends and youth group behind, and this may be especially challenging to recreate. But why is this so challenging for us? When one of my sons transitioned into high school, he found that he was not connecting as well with the friends he had grown up with. Most of the friends he had spent time with when he was younger were family relationships that my wife and I had helped to develop through shared gatherings and activities. He began to realize the need to develop his own relationships outside of the "family circle" of friends. However, he still worked to do this *within* the context of us, his parents; he drew on our resources and used our home as the general environment to broaden and deepen his new relationships. There were many nights when Sarah and I hosted and cooked for teenagers we'd never met. These people were often "friends of friends," or people our son had met through activities or youth group. We spent weekends at the lake, driving one guy after another as they learned to wakesurf or ski or just had fun tubing. Our son's effort to initiate new relationships was supported by the hospitality and resources of his parents. With our help, he was able to develop new relationships and have strong relationships with core friends.

In college, it is unlikely that you will have the immediate support of a core group of friends to help develop relationships. Nor will you have the common ground of growing up in the same area. Every conversation will be new, every experience you have with friends will be a "first time" with little shared context to draw from. The process can be exciting and daunting simultaneously. Nouwen says it this way: "you might have felt [loneliness] as a young adult in a university where everyone talked about grades but where a good friend was hard to find."[6]

There were times in each of my educational experiences when I felt a gnawing sense of loneliness and disconnection with others. The small talk and banter of new friendships began to wear thin and I longed for deep community with others who "got me" and could relate easily to me. Tim Keller echoes this in his writing about the prodigal son when he asserts, "there is no way you will be able to grow spiritually apart from a deep involvement in a community of other believers. You can't live the Christian life without a band of Christian friends, without a family of believers in which you find a place."[7] You need a band of Christians to walk through college with. God can certainly provide this, but you need to be on the lookout for it when you get there. In the first few months of college, it will be good to go to as many events put on by faith and church groups as you can—even when you don't feel like it. Make yourself go. Some will be a fit and others won't, but either way, you will be broadening your circle of friends and investing in a community that will offer support and encouragement to you in the years ahead.

Research by author Andy Crouch shows that core groups of friends often start with three central people that fan out into groups of 12 and then larger groups from there. Three is a good place to start with friends, especially when you are forming new ones. Andy believes that "culture always starts small"[8] and he encourages followers to "Find community, a small group who can lovingly fuel your dreams and puncture your illusions. Find friends and form a family who are willing to see grace at work in one another's lives, who can discern together which gifts and which crosses each has been called to bear.... Find some partners in the wild and wonderful world beyond church doors."[9] Being able to see God's grace at work is not something that comes naturally to everyone, but when you find someone who can speak this into your life, thank them and develop the relationship. They will remind you that Christ provides new starts, that you are more than your struggles, and will encourage you when you are living in your gifting. I love Andy's encouragement to consider people beyond the church door. Some of the most life-giving groups in our lives have been pulled from people who have a variety of church backgrounds.

A lot of it comes down to common interests and a shared worldview. Common interests are important because they make life interesting. I have a friend who loves to play strategy board games. He goes to a conference once a year to engage with others who share his interest. I respect my friend's passion, but cannot imagine doing it myself. However, if you put me on a ski slope with some buddies I will try to be the first one on the chairlift in the morning and the last one off in the afternoon. Pursuing common interests with others really does form a bond that will help you get to know people. Just look at the college groups that form on campus from outdoor clubs, to political groups, to sports clubs—all of them are designed to connect you with others you can relate to.

Shared worldviews are also important in cultivating new friendships. People who share your core values and beliefs will likely be the people you feel most comfortable connecting with and investing in. Churches or campus ministries can be a great place to find people who share your values. At Vanderbilt, my core group of friends came through Reformed University Fellowship (RUF). When I got to Indiana University, I plugged in with Greek Intervarsity. In both cases, I developed life-long friends who have helped keep me accountable and with whom I have shared many recreational experiences. People who share your beliefs can come from a variety of backgrounds and do not necessarily need to align with everything you have experienced. Be open to how God might lead you in seeking out friends.

It is also important that you seek out mentors who can offer encouragement and perspective from being just a few years ahead of you. My wife was mentored by a woman named Paige Benton through RUF. Paige had an incredible gift for speaking into the hearts and lives of kids in college. She would ask direct questions about my wife's thinking or patterns of behavior. One of her best pieces of advice was that you cannot sit on the fence as a Christian. You are either progressing in your faith or you are drifting away from God. Over the years, Sarah and I have come back to her words again and again, and they certainly ring true regardless of the situation.

Pushing past the feelings of discomfort and the initial awkwardness of making new friendships will be really important as you get started in college. Aligning with friends who share common hobbies and worldviews, even if it is only a few, will serve you well as you develop and grow into an adult. As Fred Rogers so aptly described, "the connections we make in the course of a life—maybe that's what heaven is."[10]

Recognizing Glimpses of Glory

Once you've aligned with some people to walk alongside of you during college, they will help you develop more fully into who God created you to be. C. S. Lewis says, "In each of my friends there is something that only some other friend can fully bring out. By myself I am not large enough to call the whole man into activity; I want other lights than my own to show all the facets."[11]

We all reflect Christ in different ways. As a friend, part of your role is to encourage others to live out their gifting—to speak into it when you see a friend come fully alive and embrace God's greatness in their life. No two friends will do it the same way. But here is the catch—it is really hard to do this if you get caught up in either (1) constantly comparing yourself with your friends or (2) seeking out the "perfect friend" who will meet all your needs and never disappoint you. These tendencies get in the way of fully embracing the glory of God in others.

What often prevents me from reaching out to people and connecting with them is my tendency to compare myself to others. Here is what frequently happens internally when I attend a gathering. I walk into a group and quickly survey the crowd. I determine who I want to talk with based on their appearance and what I may know about them. There are those I perceive could help me "get to the next level" in my pursuits; others I will try to avoid, because they may monopolize my time in an "unproductive" way; and still other people I don't know at all but all the same I've decided to either approach or not approach based largely on externals or quick interactions. The conversations ensue as the event progresses. Afterward, I reflect on my conversations—what I could have done differently, and often, how I "stack" up related to everyone else. I evaluate, judge and feel better or worse about myself based on what I learned from the night.

But at their core, these comparisons are rooted in pride. When we compare ourselves with someone else, we either determine we are better or worse than that person for whatever particular reason we contrive. We are prideful in what we have when compared to them and so we feel better about ourselves. Conversely, we see something in them we want and think we deserve to have. This feeling is a pride of entitlement—thinking we deserve to have what we see in someone else.[12]

This sort of comparison mindset will become especially challenging in college, because you will be surrounded by the same group of people. Life becomes entrenched with your classmates and you start to know everything they do, which makes comparison that much easier. Fight the tendency to compare, accept the person for who they are and try to be fully present in who God has created you to be. As Lewis says, "even in social life, you will never make a good impression on other people until you stop thinking about what sort of an impression you are making ... give yourself up, and you will find your real self. Lose your life and you will save it."[13]

Women are prone to comparing themselves to other women, especially physically. Many women look around the room to see who is the best looking, and what the other women are wearing. I hear women actually dress to impress other women. Cattiness never really goes away. It just takes a more subtle form in the workplace and the neighborhood after girls grow up. High school can be brutal as girls tend to be vicious, but college does seem to get a little better. Improving the situation in college comes down to a disciplined thought life. Accepting who you are and loving others for where they are instead of comparing yourself.

My wife is masterful at reaching beyond these tendencies to truly "love on" others, and a lot of this was developed during her college years. She was constantly befriending and sticking up for girls who seemed to be lonely or outside of social circles. One of my wife's closest friends in college came to Vanderbilt without any connections. Sarah met her on her dorm hall and they immediately hit it off. Throughout four years of college, Sarah introduced her to other friends and included her in activities. Sarah's friend ended up rooming with some of the other friends and developed supportive, ongoing relationships with them. We have enjoyed seeing her play an active role in many weddings and events over the years since college. Sarah still does this today and it always amazes and challenges me when I see her "love on" others in this way.

On a few occasions, I have approached events differently. I stay in the car for an extra minute before walking into the event—asking God to provide me with his vantage point on the room—to help me to see who is hurting in the room and look beyond all of the externals that typically bog me down and hijack my internal dialogue. The result of such a reorientation is usually quite noticeable. I find myself engaging with people at a deeper level, genuinely caring about their stories and seeking their good instead of my own. It is not perfect by a long shot, but when I move from comparing to connecting it allows me to see God in them and their story in a way that I never could with a different heart orientation.

The second tendency that can get in the way of seeing God's glory in others and encouraging authentic relationships is looking for the perfect friend. I am sure that each of us would readily admit that no perfect friend exists, but our actions and thought patterns often betray us.

God has blessed me with a good friend, Nate, who has been part of our journey for several years. We align on many levels—vocationally, spiritually and recreationally. In fact many people who casually know us just assume we are friends because of all the overlap and commonality. Yet as my wife and I have gotten close to Nate and his wife, we have had hurt feelings and miscommunications that have taken time and effort to resolve ranging from parenting styles, to coordinating summer schedules, to how groups we are in are led and structured. It is like we swing and miss even though we are both genuinely trying not to swing and miss. It has created tension on many levels, which has frustrated both of us.

As I reflected on the sources of the tension, I realized I was being perfectionistic in my expectations of him and not admitting my own part in creating the conflict. I was discouraged by the blind spots I was projecting onto him. In short, my own unrealistic expectations and judgmental tendencies were killing the relationship. I had to acknowledge my own sin, confess it and move away from it. In Nouwen's words:

No friend or lover, no husband or wife, no community or commune will be able to put to rest our deepest cravings for unity and wholeness. And by burdening others with these divine expectations, of which we ourselves are often only partially aware, we might inhibit the expression of free friendship and love and evoke instead feelings of inadequacy and weakness.[14]

As Nouwen suggests, I wanted to find wholeness and a genuine sense of belonging in Nate. Someone who could totally understand me and not let me down. By burdening Nate with all of these unspoken expectations we both felt inadequate and the relationship was strained.

Once I became aware of this, I extended grace to him and admitted my own sin. Nate and I reached a new level in our relationship. I started to value him for his own strengths, of which there are many, instead of finding fault. I started to compliment him more on his keen abilities to chart the course, figure out logistics and rally the troops around a common goal. In short, I tried to let him be free to be who God made him to be instead of trying to fit him into my perception of how I wanted him to relate. We were at an event together with a gathering of strong men of faith who were also significant business leaders in our city. Amidst all the people, Nate introduced me to the speaker as one of his very best friends. It was like time stopped for me when he said it. I honestly couldn't believe he was saying it about me until I realized I felt the same about Nate. Moving past my own sin and selfishness led me to a new place of understanding and depth in community. Our relationship certainly has not been perfect since then, but it has been more authentic and genuinely supportive. God has blessed you with unique talents and abilities that only you have, but at times you may not even be able to see them in yourself. He tells us that we are each made in His image (Genesis 1:27) and that He takes great delight our individual gifts and talents (Romans 12:6). We all reflect Him in different ways and offer glimpses into the infinite creativity and glory of who He is. Your friends will speak into that glory and bring it out in you more fully, and you will call out their gifting as well. By avoiding the temptation to compare yourself or to seek out perfection in your friends, you will be able to engage and pursue authenticity in your relationships.

Making Community a Theme

In the first decade after leaving my parents' home, I lived in sixteen different locations in less than a decade. The moves were often motivated by advances in my career or in education, but nevertheless Sarah and I moved a lot. With all of these moves, we found it was hard to build community. Dr. Keith Douds, a noted psychologist and family friend, makes community a theme in his counsel to families because it is so often overlooked and not prioritized. Without someone to continually remind you to make it a priority, you will find yourself saying yes to a variety of activities that will not foster this core sense of community. There are at least four keys I have found to making community a theme.

Give it Time

When we lived in Dallas, the people we attended church with and worked with were warm and welcoming. However, there was an underlying mindset that they would accept you if you were going to stay and become a Texan, but if not, they would not really let you in. As it turned out, they may have been right because I finished seminary and we moved across the country. Building community takes time and intentionality and there is not really a shortcut to the process.

Commit

During our time in Texas, I attended seminary and the administrative staff very intentionally put us into small groups to try to provide support in walking through the two years. We had a wonderful curriculum and met faithfully, but the group never seemed to connect very well. I think it was because we had not self-selected into the group. We were told we had to do it and somehow that changed the motivation and willingness to be vulnerable. In contrast to this group, we created a cooking group with a few couples almost a decade ago based on a shared interest and mutual commitment. We took the time to thoughtfully name the group when we started it, and since then, we intentionally come up with themes for the meals we prepare together and for our conversations. The group continues to meet quarterly and has provided life-giving support and perspective for all of us. We come prepared and ready to engage in each of our gatherings, and we invest our time and resources to make them happen.

Engage

For most people, community doesn't just happen. Plato quoted Socrates in his *Apologia*: "The life which is unexamined is not worth living." Your community will help you examine your life to determine what is working and not working and how you can more clearly hear God's voice.

We're also in a book discussion group that meets each quarter. The gatherings are usually four to six hours long and usually involve a real level of vulnerability and sharing. However, sometimes the gatherings stay in the shallow waters and do not touch the core of who we are. This can happen because members are not prepared or people do not feel like sharing authentically or the leader does not push people to go deeper. Regardless, when this happens, we walk away feeling unsatisfied. It often comes down to one person choosing to be vulnerable first and others following—one person to ask the hard questions, to foster the conversations and invite other people into it. You can fill your schedule with activities and connection points, but if you do not show up and engage when you get there, you will miss out on the rich community that could have been yours.

Create Shared Experiences

Relationships are built through shared experiences and recreation. My wife and I got to know each other through the ski trips we took in college. Being outside and doing something a little risky created the space and atmosphere that allowed us to bond in a way we never would have just hanging out at Vanderbilt. Seek out unique experiences and don't be afraid to initiate them if no one else does. C. S. Lewis reflects appropriately on shared experiences and our ability to appreciate others in his book, *The Four Loves*.

In a perfect Friendship this Appreciative Love is, I think, often so great and so firmly based that each member of the circle feels, in his secret heart, **humbled before all the rest.** Sometimes he wonders **what he is doing there** among his betters. He is **lucky beyond desert to be in such company.** Especially when the whole group is together, each bringing out all that is **best, wisest, or funniest** in all the others. Those are the **golden sessions**; when four of five of us after a hard day's walking have to come to our inn; when our slippers are on, our feet spread out towards the blaze and our drinks at our elbows; when the **whole world, and something beyond the world,** opens itself to our minds as we talk; and no one has any claim or any responsibility for another, but all **are freemen and equals** as if we had first met an hour ago, while at the same time an Affection mellowed by the years enfolds us. Life—**natural life—has no better gift to give. Who could have deserved it?** [Emphasis mine.][15]

Be Mindful of the Inner Dialogue

We all have an inner dialogue that comes from one of three sources—yourself, the Enemy or God. Being aware of the inner dialogue you bring into community will be important for you to fully connect. In her research, professor and author Brené Brown has found two tendencies that can hinder our ability to relate to each other. We sabotage ourselves by "looking for confirmation that (1) we do not belong or (2) that we're not enough."[16] When you walk into a setting, it is easy to quickly go to an inner dialogue about not belonging such as, *these people are more spiritual, better dressed, or more engaged in the group than I will ever be.* When you think you do not belong, you start to distance yourself or use it as an excuse to check out and not engage with the group. The second negative thought process that is easy to fall into is that we are not enough—*I do not have what it takes to engage with this group, I do not have the right credentials (why am I even here?)* or *I have nothing to offer this group.* Again, the result is the same—we distance ourselves and lose our ability to engage with those who may very well lead us to Christ.

The musical *Wicked* takes you behind the scenes of the Wicked Witch from the *Wizard of Oz.* One of the central themes of the story is the relationship between Glinda, the Good Witch, and Elphaba, the Wicked Witch. Toward the end of the musical, there is a pivotal scene when Elphaba finally acknowledges that she needs Glinda's gifting and talents in addition to her own.

Elphaba:

I'm limited.

Just look at me.

I'm limited.

And just look at you.

You can do all I couldn't do.

Glinda:

I've heard it said,

That people come into our lives

For a reason

Bringing something we must learn.

And we are led to those

Who help us most to grow if we let them.

And we help them in return.

Well, I don't know if I believe that's true

But I know I'm who I am today

Because I knew you.

Glinda and Elphaba together:

Because I knew you

I have been changed for the good.[17]

Glinda and Elphaba could not be who they are without each other. Glinda is called to lead the people and provide positivity and hope while Elphaba creates depth and real purpose. They each have their own gifting and shine brighter when they use their gifting in tandem. And so it goes with all the great stories—Luke needs Solo, Frodo needs Sam, Aramis needs Porthos. God is the Trinity, and the early disciples drew strength from each other to spread the message of Christ in a hostile world. We are called to align with others, appreciate their gifting as distinct from our own and make a community. Don't be frustrated by the process: in the end, it will be worth the effort. Like Aramis, something about you may 'cease to exist' when a good friend dies or moves on. Yet, the reality is "that something" may have never existed without that person's role in your life—without them calling out God's glory in you and you calling it out in them.

Discussion / Reflection Questions

1. What is your attitude toward others? Do you view them as competition or as a means to an end?

2. How can true and deep friendships bless our lives during the good seasons and the bad?

3. What do you think it takes to form strong and lasting relationships?

Chapter 17

Lean into Difficulties

"I wish it need not have happened in my time," said Frodo. "So do I,"
said Gandalf, "and so do all who live to see such times. But that is not
for them to decide. All we have to decide is what to do with the time
that has been given to us."

J. R. R. Tolkien, *The Fellowship of the Ring*

Life is not always so rosy as we might like. Dorothy set out on the yellow brick road on a high, being sent off by a whole village of cheering munchkins and after destroying one of the worst enemies in Oz. And then she encounters a terrifying lion, evil flying monkeys and a wicked witch. Prince Caspian sets out to find the lost lords, buoyed by hope, provisions for the trip and a kingdom of well-wishers, only to encounter trial after trial along the way. Hard times will come. The challenge is what we will do with them. But do you know one of the great secrets of hard times? There are no great stories without them. If Dorothy followed the yellow brick road without a single problem, it would be just a statement: A girl and her dog travelled along the yellow brick road. Likewise, if the lost lords were not lost and Caspian did not have to overcome many trials to find them, then there would be no story about Caspian. It is the difficulties themselves and how a character responds to them that make a story worth returning to over and over. So what is God doing in the story of your life and through the difficulties you encounter? How can we choose to believe God is for us even when it may not feel like it?

We looked at Jeremiah earlier, but his story is relevant to revisit. Jeremiah was a prophet who devoted his life to a message that people ultimately never responded to. He called the nation of Israel to turn from their sin, to turn from their worship of idols and false gods that had led them away from God. He even predicted the seventy years of exile the people were about to experience—they would be conquered by a foreign army and taken from the home they loved to live in a land ruled by a pagan king. Think about how long that is—seventy years in a foreign land—quadruple the years you've been around. Many people were going to die in exile. They were going to be ridiculed and mistreated by their conquerors. Yet in the midst of this darkness, God promised the people that they would have a hope and a future. Maybe not hope in the way they envisioned it, such as relief from their struggles, but a hope stemming from the good that God would bring through their trial and from the revealing of his consistent presence in their lives.

> Build houses and live *in them*; and plant gardens and eat their produce. Take wives and become the fathers of sons and daughters, and take wives for your sons and give your daughters to husbands, that they may bear sons and daughters; and multiply there and do not decrease. Seek the welfare of the city where I have sent you into exile, and pray to the LORD on its behalf; for in its welfare you will have welfare (Jeremiah 29:5-7).

God wanted these people in exile to lean into their lives even if they were not exactly as they wanted them to be at that moment. By leaning in, I mean God wanted them to invest in the city, deepen their relationships and make the most of the opportunities before them while they were in exile. The temptation would have been to wait until times improved—until they got back to the land they wanted to live in, around familiar settings and people. But that is not what he challenged them to do. He did not want them to wait. He wanted them to lean in right where they were—to invest and plant and grow.

When hard times come, resist the tendency to ask, *Why me?* Instead ask God, *What can I learn? How can I lean into this?* Or as Dan Sullivan says, "Always make your learning bigger than your experience."[1] We will all undergo difficult things in life. Will you take the time to reflect on them, to seek out what God may be telling you in the midst of the challenge? Aaron Brockett, Lead Pastor at Traders Point Christian Church, recently challenged us by acknowledging that everyone is going to have valleys / hard times. The question is whether you are going to just *Go* through the valleys or if you will *Grow* through them.[2]

Consider how simply enduring difficulties without complaining provides a light and an example for others. James 1:2–4 states it plainly: "Consider it pure joy, my brothers and sisters, whenever you face trials of many kinds, because you know that the testing of your faith produces perseverance. Let perseverance finish its work so that you may be mature and complete, not lacking anything" (NIV). What a tremendous vision: to be mature and complete, not lacking anything. God tells us that true maturity is only possible by walking through hard times.

My dad was an entrepreneur in every sense of the word. He was on a constant quest to learn, grow and develop. He began his career working for others and quickly realized that he wanted to control his own career and set his own course, and he certainly did. God led him to start a homebuilding company that eventually became the tenth largest private builder in the country. Our family business served more than 25,000 clients over twenty-five years of business by building dream homes that first-time buyers could actually afford. Our goal was to provide more home than people imagined possible —bigger bedrooms, huge game rooms and walk-in closets you could get lost in. It was a cool vision and cool to watch the excitement on people's faces when they moved in to their new homes. However, my favorite part about the company was the people who worked there. My dad always believed in hiring people who were better than him—and it showed.

What do I mean by that? What's so important about hiring 'people who are better than you'? Well, I mean that as leaders, we often compare ourselves to others and become intimidated when we don't measure up. When we see someone who is more talented than we are, or gifted in a unique way, it's far easier to get jealous and insecure than it is to admire the cool ways that God has gifted others. This is certainly true in my life. Recently, I went to a lunch with Christian leaders in the Indianapolis area. At the lunch, a guy I know was asked to give the blessing. On the spot, he prayed an amazingly powerful, eloquent and succinct prayer over our time together. As I sat and listened, do you know what I felt? Jealousy. I thought to myself, *why can't I stand up and pray like that?* Chuck Swindoll recently told me that he got rid of jealousy early on in his career and that's how he's managed to be successful. "Know yourself, accept yourself and be yourself," he said. And it's that middle step of accepting who you are that is the key. Accept how God has made you and be just that. Ask yourself, *How do I use God's gifting to the highest of my ability?* Accepting what you are and what you are not frees you to be happy and amazed at the way God has gifted others. When I walked away from the lunch, I turned to the guy who had given the prayer and told him he was uniquely gifted with words, and I appreciated the way he had blessed us by using his gifting. His face lit up and he was beaming as he thanked me for the compliment. If I had not realized my own jealousy and fought the game inside my head—or not taken the thought captive (2 Corinthians 10:5)—we both would have missed out on the way God wanted to encourage and bless us that day.

That's how my dad was. Instead, of measuring himself against all the awesome people he met, he allowed himself to be amazed by their gifting and focused on the real task of getting them to come work for him! His business was full of people who were "better" than him because he never let his ego get in the way—and, as I said, it really showed. People loved working there. There were so many weddings and so many children that came along as a result of people meeting at that company. Even today— a decade later—former employees still arrange get-togethers and catch-ups. There is still a Facebook page where they all connect. It was an exciting culture to be a part of because the quality of the people who worked there was so high.

Business was good too. One year, the company was the title sponsor for the Indianapolis Colts, back when Peyton Manning was quarterback and Tony Dungy was coach and the Colts were all anyone talked about in town. I remember sitting in some unbelievable seats and watching our family's name flash across the screen at a game. We worked hard to build the brand, and pretty much everyone in the city had at least heard about the company. They either loved us for the opportunities we created for them or they hated us because they didn't like the product or were jealous of the success. Either way, there was a definite notoriety that came from being part of a successful family business.

Then the housing bubble burst, and the world seemed to change overnight.

For years all we'd talked about was how we needed to buy more land. We couldn't buy it fast enough. Then, overnight, it flipped. The banks told us we had too much land. Our greatest asset suddenly became a noose around our necks. We had 300 homebuyers signed and ready to build—there are professional builders who won't build that many houses over their entire career! But the banks were nervous. The mortgage approvals, which used to come in easily, now became difficult. Buyers started losing their jobs and defaulting on their contracts. Our business was the same as it had always been, but suddenly things were out of our control. Our family was faced with one of the hardest decisions we've had to make: either we closed down the company or we put in a huge sum of personal funds to try to keep it afloat through a recession that was just beginning.

It wasn't much of a choice. We decided to close the company. The aftermath was one of the darkest times we've walked through as a family. Unwinding a business is not an easy thing to do: aggressive attorneys and creditors want their share of the scraps; buyers who envisioned their family moving into their new community, or whose houses were already under construction, had to find new options. We also had to let all our employees go, which was probably the hardest thing of all. What made it even harder was that—even after they knew they were going to lose their jobs—most of them chose to stay on with us until the end. Even though it would have been better for them to find new employment as soon as possible, they stayed until we closed our doors. It was a terrible feeling to know you were letting down people as loyal and as good as the people who worked for us. All of this lasted for more than three years after the company closed and took a huge toll on my dad and our family.

Walking through this dark season also created a reliance on God that our family thought we had before it happened. Our identity had become wrapped up in the prestige of the company—the access it afforded to special privileges and people that others did not have, as well as financial benefits. I remember being embarrassed to say my last name and I would cringe as I watched people connect the dots about what was going on with the company. It made me realize that my identity needed to be in God and nothing else. First Timothy 6:17-19 took on new meaning: "Instruct those who are rich in this present world not to be conceited or to fix their hope on the uncertainty of riches, but on God, who richly supplies us with all things to enjoy. Instruct them to do good, to be rich in good works, to be generous and ready to share, storing up for themselves the treasure of a good foundation for the future, so that they may take hold of that which is life indeed." We had taken on an identity which was false, a sense of worth which felt solid but was instead fleeting and uncertain. God wanted to get at our hearts and reorient them toward Himself. He was not afraid to pull down our strongholds to accomplish His purpose.

And do you know what? God may do this to you, too, eventually. I'm not talking about a family business closing, because that might not be your situation. What I mean is that whatever you rely on—no matter what it is—may come crumbling down and force you to rely on God more than yourself. The question is what will be the orientation of your heart when you are walking through it? What does God want you to do when that happens? He wants you to lean into the difficulty.

But good came from that experience as well, though it was hard for my family and me to see at the time. In the end, it pushed me, and each of my siblings, into our own callings. When you have a successful family company, there is a sense of stewardship or obligation, a strong pull toward being involved in the business. As the only son in my family, I felt I needed to be there for my dad. I was convinced that the role I'd been put on earth to play was taking up my dad's mantle and making sure the company continued beyond his generation. But if I'm honest with myself, my heart was not in it. I certainly have some similarities with my dad, but ultimately we are wired very differently. Had the company not closed down, I would have never felt the freedom to pursue starting my companies and serving older adults and the elderly. Neither would I have experienced a lot of other aspects of my life that bring meaning and purpose to me and which God uses to bless me and others.

One of the most impactful moments of my vocational life was when I met with a very influential family who had just about everything that most people dream of. They were incredibly blessed, and yet when I sat down with the matriarch of the family to discuss how we could come alongside and support them, I sensed a deep sadness in her. After talking for more than an hour, she finally turned to me and said, "David, can you please send someone who can help give me purpose in my life again? My family and friends are very nice, but I just don't want to live to get another year older." It was a watershed moment for me. I realized the immense amount of trust and honor this family was placing in us. To be able to send people who could provide meaning and purpose toward the end of someone's life is a really significant calling.

Building houses like my dad did is great, but helping people create active and engaged lives through exceptional care as they get older is something that makes me feel fulfilled and passionate. And I would never have been able to do it if my dad's company was still around. I would have been dutiful to him and the family and I would have continued working there, all the while losing myself little by little. The company he built was his dream, not mine. When the company closed, it freed me to chart my own course, which has made all the difference, even though I would never have guessed I'd end up where I am.

In Romans 8, Paul compels us to have a heart that believes God is for us even in the dark times:

> Who will separate us from the love of Christ? Will tribulation, or distress, or persecution, or famine, or nakedness, or peril, or sword? … But in all these things we overwhelmingly conquer through Him who loved us. For I am convinced that neither death, nor life, nor angels, nor principalities, nor things present, nor things to come, nor powers, nor height, nor depth, nor any other created thing, will be able to separate us from the love of God, which is in Christ Jesus our Lord (Romans 8:35, 37–39).

God is for you. You have likely already walked through some hard times and you will again, but having the right orientation during those hard times is really important.

Horatio Spafford wrote one of the most beloved hymns of all times, "It is Well with My Soul." It's a beautiful song that has encouraged generations of Christians. But have you ever wondered about the story behind such powerful words and music? It's worth looking into.

Spafford was an accomplished Chicago lawyer and businessman with a lovely family. However, the Spaffords were not strangers to setbacks in life. Their young son died of pneumonia in 1871, and in that same year much of their business was lost in the great Chicago fire. Yet God allowed the business to flourish once more.

On November 21, 1873, Mrs. Spafford and their four daughters were on board a ship crossing the Atlantic. Mr. Spafford had planned to go with his family, but he had to stay behind to help solve an unexpected business problem. He planned to take another ship and join his family in Europe a few days later. About four days into the crossing of the Atlantic, the ship collided with another vessel, and in an instant everyone on board was in grave danger. It is reported that Anna brought her four children to the deck and prayed for help from God. Within approximately twelve minutes, the ship slipped beneath the dark waters of the Atlantic, carrying with it 226 of the passengers, including the four Spafford children.

A sailor, rowing a small boat over the spot where the ship went down, saw a woman floating on a piece of wreckage. It was Anna, and she was miraculously still alive. He helped her into his boat and from there she journeyed to Wales where she wired her husband, "Saved alone, what shall I do?"

Another of the ship's survivors, Pastor Weiss, later recalled Anna saying, "God gave me four daughters. Now they have been taken from me. Someday I will understand why."

Mr. Spafford got on the next available ship and left to join his grieving wife. The captain called Spafford to his cabin and told him when they were over the place where the ship with his children went down. It was at that moment that the words to "It is Well with My Soul" came to Horatio's mind.[3]

Delivering *Your* Future

When peace like a river attendeth my way,

When sorrows like sea billows roll,

Whatever my lot, Thou has taught me to say,

It is well, it is well with my soul.[4]

Horatio got it. In the midst of trials, he realized and acknowledged that God was still in control. He grieved and, no doubt, felt all of the emotions, yet he maintained belief in the sovereignty of God. He trusted that God had a plan and a purpose for what was happening, and he trusted in Him more than in his circumstances.

The challenge is to lean into the hard times, and to not try to straighten the curves along the way. Try to stay with the pain. Seek out what can be learned and do your best to walk through suffering with dignity and grace. God will use your story to influence and encourage those around you. It is often the bruises that we get during these setbacks that provides purpose and meaning. The lyrics from Train's song "Bruises" say it well:

These bruises make for better conversation
Loses the vibe that separates
It's good to let you in again
You're not alone in how you've been
Everybody loses, we all got bruises
We all got bruises ...

I would love to fix it all for you
I would love to fix you too
Please don't fix a thing whatever you do

Discussion / Reflection Questions

1. What is your reaction to pain? Do you avoid it? Wallow in it? Why?

2. What have you learned from walking through challenges in the past? How have you seen growth?

3. You will likely encounter something hard in the next twenty-four hours. Take a moment and ask God to help you have a right heart orientation and attitude when trouble comes.

Chapter 18

Fight against Lust

When I get honest, I admit I am a bundle of paradoxes. I believe and doubt, I hope and get discouraged, I love and feel hate, I feel bad about feeling good ... I say I am an angel with an incredible capacity for beer.

Brennan Manning, *Ragamuffin Gospel*

In *The Voyage of the Dawn Treader*, Prince Caspian seeks to rediscover the lost lords of Narnia. Throughout the journey, each of the main characters encounters very real temptations that get at a particular area of vulnerability in his or her heart. Lucy is confronted with idolizing her older sister's beauty. She desperately wants to be like her. In a trance, Lucy imagines that she has become Susan but quickly finds that giving in to her fantasy leaves her feeling hollow and empty about herself.

Lucy's brother, Peter, faces the temptation of wanting power over Prince Caspian. He was the High King of Narnia—many years ago—and he now finds it difficult to submit to Caspian's authority. He has to work through his inordinate desire for power in order to appreciate his own gifting and that of Caspian. Through each of the characters, C. S. Lewis shows that before you can fight the evil outside, you must fight the evil inside. In college, you will have to wrestle the evil inside of you, which may come in the form of sexual desire.

Delivering *Your* Future

If you grew up with parents who encouraged you to follow God, you've probably heard about the "big sins" of drugs, sex and alcohol. However, God views all sins the same because any sin takes our hearts further away from communion and connection with Him. James tells us that if you commit murder but do not commit adultery, not only have you broken the Law of God but you are guilty of breaking all of it (James 2:11-13). It really does not matter how you sin; if you transgress even one of God's perfect standards—desiring something a friend has, telling a lie to your parents—you are just as guilty as if you had committed a "big" sin.

Although all sins pull us away from God in a way that saddens Him deeply, there are most certainly different consequences for our sin. You may never be forcefully reprimanded for a fight with one of your siblings, but if you break in and steal from someone, you will face years of prison time. Are both wrong? Sure. But one delivers far greater consequences than the other. My point is that while this chapter is focused on lust, I am not singling it out because it is somehow worse than other sins. I know men and women who've been trapped in sexual sins for years and those who have sold their souls to the pursuit of generating wealth: they both seem equally lost after years of bowing down to their respective sins. A Lewis puts it, "a greedy, backstabbing, self-righteous person could often be further away from God than a prostitute."[1] The reason we are delving into physical and sexual sin more closely is because when you are in your late teens and early twenties, your hormones are still raging. Your body is fully developed and ready to reproduce, and if you had lived 100 years ago you probably would have been married with kids at your age. College gives you more freedom to experiment and explore than ever before. The social scene, feelings of autonomy, lack of personal history in a new location, and your peers will all likely encourage physical intimacy and sexual exploration more than ever before.

Recognize How Alluring Sexual Sin Can Be

The Bible addresses sexual immorality in 1 Corinthians 6:18: "Flee from sexual immorality. All other sins a person commits are outside the body, but whoever sins sexually sins against their own body," (NIV). Giving into lust could mean taking a longer look at someone you are attracted to, going further physically than you intended to with someone, looking at pornography, fantasizing while masturbating, or having sex outside of marriage. Each of these are sins against your own body that will have more lasting effects than you anticipate. The images and experiences you have in this arena will stay with you longer and will control you more than other sins you commit that are outside of your body. Every time you give yourself physically to something or someone else, a memory is created that is not easily replaced or forgotten. You will bring all of these experiences into your marriage and it will affect your perception of what physical intimacy should look like in marriage.

C.S. Lewis in *Mere Christianity* makes the point that giving in to a sexual appetite can be bigger and more far reaching than other appetites. He comments that "the appetite is in ludicrous and preposterous excess of its function"[2] and that sexual sin, like any sin, grows with indulgence. The more you give in to it the more it will take hold of your life and threaten the relationships that are important to you. Giving in to sexual sins can be an addiction just like a substance addiction. Your body becomes dependent on it and it is hard to break free from it. Just like an addiction to drugs, it can often take a "bigger hit" the next time to get the same "high." This results in an ever-increasing negative cycle that can often take hold of your thought life and behavior.

Appreciate Sex as God Intended

Before we go into some practical ways you can fight lust in college, let's pause and reflect on the way God designed sex and how he made it to be good. Rather than the physical experimentation and cheap one-night stands that our culture promotes, God wants us to enjoy sex in the context of a man and woman in a marriage relationship. "For this reason a man will leave his father and mother and be united to his wife, and the two shall become one flesh" (Ephesians 5:3). In his book, *The Meaning of Marriage*, pastor Timothy Keller expands on God's intention for sex.

> Is sex dirty and demeaning as others have said? No. Biblical Christianity may be the most body-positive religion in the world. It teaches that God made matter and physical bodies and saw that it was all good (Genesis 1:31).... The Bible contains great love poetry that celebrates sexual passion and pleasure. If anyone says that sex is bad or dirty in itself, we have the entire Bible to contradict him.[3]

Sex is good because God made it good. It is in our basic DNA to want to re-create and produce offspring, so don't beat yourself up for having the desire for intimacy and sex. The desire for sex is natural and God-ordained.

If we accept that sex is good and something to be anticipated and desired, the goal becomes to make it through college and keep yourself pure as an act of obedience to God and to protect your intimacy with your future spouse. Once you get married, you will have the freedom to express yourself sexually in the context of a committed and loving relationship. Marriage will provide the safety and security to truly be vulnerable with each other and enjoy sex as God designed it. It is something to look forward to and very much worth all of the effort and prayer it will take to get there over the next few years.

Watch Your Eyes

Sexual sin usually starts with wandering eyes. An example would be a lingering gaze at someone across the classroom which then turns into fantasizing about that person. Or feeling lonely and wanting to procrastinate from studying late and finding yourself clicking on a few ads or images online. Going to see a movie that you're pretty sure features a sex scene. If you're honest, your mind may come back to those scenes and they will influence your view of sex and your need for intimacy.

My wife and I were once invited to spend time with another couple as part of a church group to talk about improving marriage. The evening we attended was focused on physical intimacy and the couple was really transparent about how they had grown their physical relationship over thirty-five years of marriage. In a breakout session with just the men, the husband talked about his struggle with pornography. He admitted that after being exposed to pornography at an early age, it had always seemed normal—almost encouraged—that as a man he was entitled to watch pornography. During his college days, in his fraternity it was normal to view and share pornography. Since then, he'd struggled with pornography for twenty years.

His experience is not uncommon for most men. Stephen Arterburn shares similar patterns from his own life and those he has counseled in his book, *Every Man's Battle*. It is a helpful resource if you feel trapped in this struggle. For women, *No Stones: Women Redeemed from Sexual Addiction* by Marnie C. Ferree is a good resource. Pornography is a slippery slope and once you start down the slope, it is hard to get off of it. Among the biggest problems that a porn addiction brings to a committed relationship or marriage is that it absolutely debilitating for the partner who does not struggle with the addiction.

One of John and Stasi Eldredge's themes in their writings about men and women is that women want to have a beauty to unveil. Stasi's book *Captivating* expands on this and is especially helpful for women in understanding how to base their self-worth on

Christ. Women want to be sought after and desired by their husbands. When a husband goes to other images or people to find what he thinks is beautiful or desirable, he is telling his wife, "You are not beautiful enough for me. You do not have what it takes to captivate me." It is a devastating assault on a woman, and the enemy will use it to create a haunting sense of doubt and uncertainty at her core. For many men, this struggle that has a huge impact on their marriages began with choices they made with their eyes in adolescence and college.

Jesus makes this very clear when He says, "You have heard that it was said, 'You shall not commit adultery'; but I say to you that everyone who looks at a woman with lust for her has already committed adultery with her in his heart" (Matthew 5:27-28). And in the next chapter, "The eye is the lamp of the body; so then if your eye is clear, your whole body will be full of light. But if your eye is bad, your whole body will be full of darkness. If then the light that is in you is darkness, how great is the darkness!" (Matthew 6:22-23). This should make us stop in our tracks. Lust starts with what you look at. The images you choose to linger over and bring back to your mind after you have seen them. The sin is committed in your heart and followed by a physical act. Your eyes can encourage your devotion to Christ or they can pull you toward the world. So how do you practically fight your eyes lingering or dwelling on images that would encourage lust in your heart?

Guard Your Thoughts

Martin Luther said, "You can't stop birds from flying over your head, but you can stop them from making a nest in your hair." In other words, sexual thoughts will come and you should not feel guilty about it, but you can choose to dwell on them or dismiss them.[4] One of the most helpful ways to push sexual sins out of your head is to fill it with God's Word. It is living and active (Hebrews 4:12). David wrote that he hid God's Word in his heart so that he would not sin against Him (Psalm 119:11). You can start really simply by having one verse that is your go-to verse which you commit to saying in your head when you are tempted to take a second look. Or challenge yourself to memorize longer passages so that when you are tempted at night, your mind has to fully concentrate to run through a whole Psalm or chapter. Psalm 1 or John 1 are good places to start. God's Word is effective in pushing back the sins that tend to form in our minds. His Word can be a shaft of light to illuminate the dark corners in your mind. But you have to read it and know it for it to work. It does not happen without discipline.

Be Intentional about Workouts

A lot of people bow down to body image, and if you go places where people like that congregate, then it will likely provide your mind with ample material to work with. You are there to work out, but if you are honest, you might admit that part of your motivation is the scenery. You have to be intentional with this area of your mind, as purposeful thinking does not just happen and might require more effort and resources from you. You will need to find a place with good equipment that is not overly crowded. It may not be quite as motivating in achieving your fitness goals, but it will do wonders at helping to protect your mind. Thinking about how you can shift your workout outside can also be helpful. God often provides renewal and a sense of purpose as you spend time in nature. Can you take a jog, cycle or take a walk in a park or along a path that provides rejuvenation instead of the congestion and distraction of a gym? I will never forget workouts when I lived in New England. It was colder and darker than the Midwest and yet people did not let it stop them from getting out and about. They bundled up and took walks, did cross-country skiing and embraced the winter. Don't let the winter stop you from getting outside and creating a sense of renewal both physically and mentally.

Pick a Cause

At one point in my life, the desire for a new car seemed to consume my thoughts. I knew every make and model that was out and I seemed bent on making it happen. At the same time, my wife and I were getting involved in a ministry in India. I decided that every time the desire to have a new car came, I would pray for the kids we had met in India. It was amazing how the power of prayer took my mind off my desire for a new car and reoriented it toward God. Prayer has the power to change our hearts in many ways, and if you prayed every time you felt sexual desire you would be amazed by its power to relieve your desires. It will help you redirect your thought life and get you out of the focus you have on yourself and your own desires in that moment.

Be Thoughtful about the Media You Consume

Hollywood has an incredible ability to make sex look blissful and without consequence. When you watch a movie or TV show that encourages sex outside of marriage, it very rarely points out the emotional turmoil that can result. And whether we realize or not, these ideas about sex have a profound influence on our own thoughts about it—if we watch turmoil-free sexual encounters all the time, we begin to believe that sex really is free of human collateral. I realize it is hard socially to not be "in the know" about certain movies or shows that come out. However, if you go to see them, decide in advance that you will look down or close your eyes during scenes that might be alluring to you. The same applies to social media; be thoughtful about what you look at and choose not to look at the sites that might pull you away. The reality is that even with the best guardrails in place, you will still encounter people and situations that will tempt you. You need to decide in advance that you will look away. Instead of lingering, choose to simply look at something else.

Recognize Patterns

Satan has been tempting humans and warring against our souls since the world began, even though we do not see the spiritual forces battling in our everyday lives (Ephesians 6:12). He has tried and proven methods that discourage us and keep us self-focused. Satan wants to distract us and get us off course any way he can. He has studied human patterns of thought and behavior since the world began. Do not be naïve. He is lurking and wants to thwart you from following God with your whole heart. "Be of sober spirit, be on the alert. Your adversary, the devil, prowls around like a roaring lion, seeking someone to devour" (1 Peter 5:8). One of the best ways he does this is to identify patterns of behavior in your life and devise appropriate temptations to go alongside them. It is possible for him to enact this plan even before you realize it's happening.

For years, I would experience a feeling of despondency and discouragement on certain evenings. I could not put my finger on it, but I would mope around and give in to a variety of distractions from food, to lust, to anger. In looking at the activities of my day, I finally realized there was often a spiritually significant event that was planned for the next day, like meeting with someone who really needed to hear about the hope of Christ or a conversation that could lead to an exponential impact in my life or ministry. It was a pattern that Satan had recognized in my own life and was exploiting. Now when I feel that way in the evenings, I ask God to give me strength and perspective for how He might use me the next day, and then I look at my calendar. I almost always find a clue. Satan wants to distract me and get me all caught up in my own inner narrative and distractions which prevent me from fully engaging in the tasks that are put before me.

In college, the pattern of temptation was almost always when I was getting my week started. Because we were at two different colleges while we were dating, my wife and I would spend the weekends together and then return to our schools. It made

Sundays really hard, because I was not only discouraged by the amount of work that loomed ahead, but also by missing the woman I loved and wanted to be with all of the time. Satan would tempt me with everything he could throw at me on those nights, and I would often give in to destructive patterns of behavior— lust, procrastination on homework, excessive eating and media intake. That would then set me up for a week of cramming and stress. Had I realized it at the time, I could have built some safeguards into my life to help combat some of it. Even telling a few buddies about it would have been a step in the right direction. Realizing the times when you are likely to be vulnerable is at least half of the battle.

Get to the Root

Another important thing to realize when you are tempted to engage in distractions like lust, but also other things like excessive alcohol, is that there is often a root issue pushing you toward this behavior. For example, if you aren't engaged in a community and seeking out people to walk through life with, you're far more likely to have feelings of loneliness which manifest as patterns of lust. The root issue is that you have a need to belong, and if you are not experiencing that, then watching pornography or "checking out the scenery" will scratch the itch for a moment. In his book on idols titled *Gospel Treason*, Brad Bigney states, "When the pressure is on, you look for quick gratification. 'I just need a hit of pleasure,' you tell yourself. This is where pornography comes in. ... You just want a quick intense self-focus so that you don't have to worry about a relationship with someone else. Pornography is false intimacy."[5] The irony is that after giving in, you will feel even more lost, hurt and vulnerable than you did before. It will not and cannot satisfy you. Ask the deeper questions. Go upstream and seek to understand why you are being tempted with this now. What unfulfilled longing or true need is pushing you to seek distraction?

Realize it Will Not Satisfy You

Author Ted Dekker's mission is "to explore truth through mind-bending stories that invite readers to see the world through a different lens. Story is the shortest distance between the human heart and truth, and to this he has devoted his life."[6] His stories reveal Christian truths through metaphor, which makes them come to life. In his epic fantasy series The Circle, there is a great, strong-willed warrior named Marak, who wants the power to defeat the opposition he faces, but instead he falls prey to sexual desire. His lust is so strong that he gives in to a relationship that ultimately takes him further away from his goals and hurts a lot of people in the process. The physical act, which seemed so alluring to Marak at first, quickly becomes tainted and dissatisfying. What once seemed pleasurable soon becomes repulsive. Does that sound familiar? So much of a sexual sin is about the anticipation—the longing for it. Once you have started the act, there is a rush of emotions and feelings, but afterwards they quickly become tainted. You're unsatisfied, yet to fill the void of emptiness you desire more of the very thing you just had—the very thing that caused you to feel dissatisfied. It never satisfies. It always leaves you empty and wanting more. For Marak, the path to destruction started—as it often does for us, too—with giving in to physical temptation.

Pastor Mark Vroegrop asks some great questions to help get to the heart of our desire to sin: "What is that one sin that you think will satisfy you? The one thing that, if you only gave in to it, you would feel happy and content? Even if you gave in, the reality is that it would not satisfy you. It would only leave you feeling disillusioned, disappointed and longing for another hit."

Get It off Your Chest

James admonishes us to "confess your sins to one another, and pray for one another so that you may be healed. The effective prayer of a righteous man can accomplish much" (James 5:16). This is especially true of sexual sins. If you have ever come home from a trip to discover food that is past its prime in your pantry, you will understand this principle. Mold grows in darkness and takes over that which was good. If you leave the food in the light or keep it out of warm, dark places, it will last a lot longer. The same is true of all sin but especially sexual sin. The more you let it fester and grow internally, the more it will take up residence in your life and heart. Find some safe friends you can confess it to and get it off your chest. Bring it into the light. Although you think you are the only one who struggles with it, you are not. You will often find the same struggles are present in others around you. You are not as alone as you thought you were. We need each other's help to carry our burdens and actively redirect each other to the throne of Christ.

Accept New Starts

"Very often what God first helps us towards is not the virtue itself but just the power of always trying again."[7] This is the essential crux of the Christian life, not that we are perfect or that we ever have it all together, but that we get up and try again. That we realize our own limitations and how God's incredible grace meets us in our places of vulnerability and despair. Here is the typical cycle of sin:

You feel discouraged, bored or listless. Some kind of a trigger emotion pushes you into self-doubt and wanting to feel a release from the patterns of daily life or pressures. Temptation either comes along or you seek it out—something to look at, or to eat or social media to consume. You give in and feel better—briefly—and then almost imme- diately you start feeling shame and guilt about what you have done. Satan rushes in and adds to the feelings by saying things like "See. That is who you are" or "You will never be able to overcome that struggle." You push these feelings aside and resolve to get back up on your feet and do better again. You can will yourself through it and make yourself stop the next time you feel tempted ... right? Maybe not.

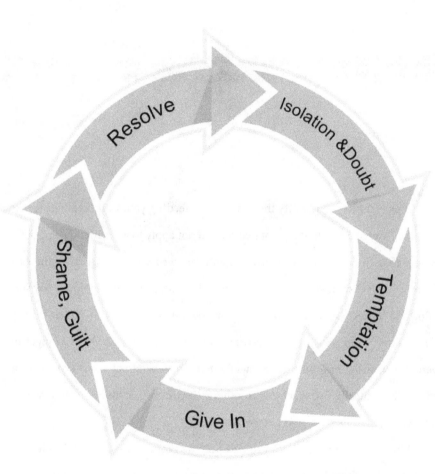

Delivering *Your* Future

The only way to break this cycle is to truly and deeply accept God's grace for you in the moment. Here is what it looks like:

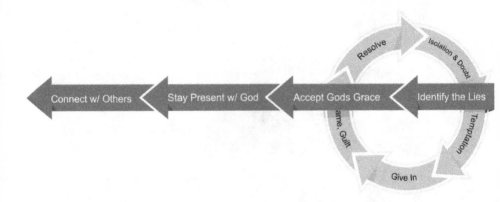

After you blow it, identify the lies Satan is feeding you. Call them out for what they are—untruths from the pit of hell that do not apply to an heir and child of God. Accept that God has truly forgiven you and removed your sins as far as the east is from the west (Psalm 103:12). Stay present with God. Stay in the moment. Say something like: *I don't know about tomorrow or even an hour from now, but right now, in this moment, I am going to stay present with God.* If you make it about a longer time period—anything beyond that moment—it starts to be about your own works and effort. Then, ideally you reach out to others, so you are not alone—people who can offer you encouragement and perspective.

With the help of the Spirit, you will become more aware of what is going on in your thought life and with your own trigger points. These trigger points will often be tied to feelings of Hunger, Anger, Loneliness or Tiredness (HALT). You can then start to redirect the cycle and avoid the behavior so that pattern looks more like the diagram on the next page. Focusing not on perfection but progress. Putting one foot in front of the other.

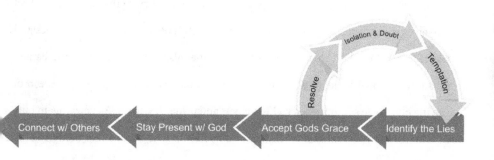

found in Luke 15. The stories of both brothers have application for how we deal with sexual sin as well as other sins. In the church, we tend to focus on the lost brother in the story who went away and squandered his inheritance and ended up eating with the pigs. We can all probably relate to this brother at some level during times of more dramatic or visible sin in our lives when we have had to turn from it. When you turn from an outward sexual sin and temptation, you can feel like the younger brother in this story.

However, Keller focuses less on the younger brother and more on the elder brother. The religious audience Christ was speaking to would have identified more with the older brother, who stayed at home and dutifully obeyed all his father instructed him to do. In the parable, this attitude is reflected in the older brother's refusal to come into the party when the younger brother returns. Instead, the older brother chooses to isolate himself by staying outside in the cold. He needed to turn from his own inward sins of jealousy, envy and self-righteousness. Keller paraphrases the epiphany we are meant to get from this story: "You mean that in order to grow in Christ, you *keep* telling yourself how graciously loved and accepted you are?"[8] And that is our challenge: to accept God's grace and provision and try anew.

Delivering *Your* Future

If we find ourselves in a younger brother place of outward sexual sin with others, we have to admit our mistakes, accept God's grace and return to the Father. If we find ourselves in more private "older brother " sin, which is often what sexual fantasies and pornography look like, then we need to admit that also and turn back to the Father. To admit our own follies and shortcomings and "come back" into the party instead of staying outside in self-imposed righteousness and pride. Try again. As Lewis again puts it: "He will not judge us as if we had not difficulties to overcome. What matters is the sincerity and perseverance of our will to overcome them."[9]

Discussion / Reflection Questions

1. Why do you think that God designed sex for marriage?

2. If you plan to fight sexual temptation in college, what do you think are the most important ways you can do that?

3. Does shame and isolation move us away from or toward God? How can we move back into His presence after we sin?

Chapter 19

Identifying Your Gifting

"For it will be like a man going on a journey, who called his servants and
entrusted to them his property. To one he gave five talents, to another two,
to another one, to each according to his ability. Then he went away."
The Parable of the Talents, Matthew 25:14-15 (esv)

Believe that God Has Gifted You

God has uniquely gifted you. He wants to use the way He has wired you to bless and encourage the world around you. Do you believe that? It can be hard to believe this sometimes—especially when you are surrounded by high achieving people who seem to have it all together. You can find yourself wanting to be like them, to fit in, or to be accepted. If you follow others' paths too long, you may wake up one day and realize you have become someone you are not. If you let him, God will use you to change the world for Him, but it is going to require some work on your part to determine what you are really good at. You have to figure out your sweet spot and look for opportunities to leverage your skills and gifting to the fullest.

For a period of my life, I was convinced that thinking through my strengths would encourage pride in my heart. After all, the Bible clearly calls us to give of ourselves to others and to think more highly of others than ourselves (Philippians 2:3). While this is certainly true, I have come to realize that having a good understanding of your gifting can actually help you live out these truths even more. For example, I (along with many other guys) may have always had the desire to play professional football. I could have pursued that dream and tried to make it a reality by working out, playing in leagues, and learning from the best players I could find, but the fact is I really did not have the build or the natural athletic ability to reach that goal. Would it have been more selfish of me to keep putting time and money into an ability that would never have developed into anything useful? Or would I have been better off to recognize the gifts I did have and seek to serve others in the best way possible with those gifts?

A friend of mine, who is a gifted counselor, once said to me, "David, I am not that good at business. I freely admit that, but I am good at relationships. I can read people and help people work through things in a way they could not on their own. Does that sound selfish?" I had to admit that it did not sound selfish at all. I thought about all the people I knew who had spent time with this counselor and all the relationships that he had helped to flourish. If he had devoted his life to business instead, many people would have missed out on the blessing he provides.

Some years back I hired a bright and talented woman, Gretchen, to join our sales team. Initially, it seemed like a good fit because of Gretchen's gregarious and outgoing personality. However, the longer she was in the role, the more discouraged she became. She was not hitting the goals we wanted her to, and we could sense her frustration. She was used to being a high contributor. Finally, we stepped back and thought about what her top three strengths were—the areas that she really excelled in. As we did, it became clear to us that she was a valuable part of the team, but just in the wrong seat— or as Walt Disney might have said, we had "cast her in the wrong role." We thought through the different roles on our team, the gaps in our performance, and determined we needed more operational strength and leadership. So we transitioned Gretchen into an operational leadership role. The change was immediate and palpable. She became a culture-maker for the team and brought energy to those around her. She was able to roll-up her sleeves, help identify problems and create solutions to issues that were bottlenecking the company in a significant way. As a result of her efforts, the company experienced great growth, and individuals working around her felt more supported and aligned than ever. It required a lot of work to figure all of this out and make the transition happen, but it was well worth the effort.

In the upcoming years, you will find that many people will help you along your journey, from college professors to friends to people who hire you. The clearer you can be with your own giftedness and where you see yourself excelling, the more people will be able to help you. The challenge is that our educational system programs kids to follow the rules and does not encourage a lot of free thought. When you graduate, it will be all about your ability to think, to pull together the threads and themes God has woven in your life and chart a meaningful path for yourself and, one day, for your family. You will want to find someone who can "unpack" your giftedness and set you on your way toward happiness and fulfillment. However, the reality is that while mentors can and will help you along the way, this role ultimately belongs to God. In His wisdom, He does not tell us the whole playbook in advance—likely because we could not handle it. Instead, He chooses to provide us with the next step along the path and then asks us to walk in faith and trust Him in the process.

We never know how God may be working behind the scenes, but we must be confident that He is. When you are leading a team of people, you can often see this as people grow and develop with opportunities. On one occasion, we had begun working with a consultant named Sam. Sam had been working for his dad's company for a number of years and was just doing consulting on the side. He and his wife had been asking God for guidance without any clear direction and were becoming frustrated and disillusioned. On one particular Sunday at church, they felt like God was calling them to change their prayers and fully give the situation to Him. It was a transformational step and one they did not take lightly. On the other side, God was identifying some gaps in our team leading me to create a new role. Just when God got Sam to the point of really trusting, we reached out to him with the opportunity. He was clear on his gifting and we were able to plug him into a role that benefited both the company and his career. God was working on our hearts and his at the same time to create an opportunity for both of us.

Our vision is so limited. We do not see clearly on this side of heaven. We have no idea how God will work in the situations around us to bring about His good purposes. But it is helpful if you have an idea of your gifting and where you might want to go with it. But how do figure this out?

Understand Gifting and Its Importance

Dan Sullivan defines a unique ability as what you love to do and do best. According to him, unique ability activities have four characteristics:

Superior Skill—You have a great talent that other people notice and value.

Passion—You love doing it and want to do it as much as possible.

Energy—It's energizing for you and others.

Never-Ending Improvement—You keep getting better / Unending growth possibilities.[1]

Sullivan proposes that the key to really growing in life is building an understanding of your own unique abilities, while also appreciating the unique abilities of those who work with you. David Rendall echoes a lot of what Dan Sullivan says by suggesting that much of our lives are spent trying to perfect our weaknesses. In school for example, you have to spend a lot of time working on the hard subjects that do not come naturally, like math for example. You are supposed to do it on your own and not rely on other people to help you. When you get out of school, it completely changes. If you are not good at math, you most certainly should not go into a profession that relies on math. Instead, you should align yourself with people who are good at math and can complement your own strengths. By focusing on your own strengths and the things that make you unique and leveraging them, you will get further in life than constantly spending time working on making marginal progress on your weaknesses.[2]

Think about Your Gifting

God takes great delight in you. He made you and He loves you with an infinite love. Recently, I was having coffee with a friend who shared a story about a group of high schoolers she works with. She asked them to raise their hands if they felt that they had ever done something that would make God not love them. She said that everyone in the room raised their hand. When we are honest, that is how many of us probably feel. The reality is that God loves you infinitely and takes great delight in the way He has uniquely wired you. God does not make mistakes.

What follows are a series of exercises that will help you to think through your gifting. We are going to walk through the exercises now. There are forms at the end of the book to help you work through them on your own. This is going to require some intentionality on your part, which means you're going to have to set aside some time and space to do this. Start by blocking out an hour somewhere in a location that you enjoy and motivates you. This could be a favorite coffee shop, a library if you are easily distracted, or maybe your own room. It will also be helpful if you ask God to guide you in this process. Start by praying before you start each of these sessions to ask God for His insight to lead you through this thought process.

Exercise 1 - Insightful Questions

Begin by taking a few minutes to answer the following questions:

- What are my top three strengths and an example of when I used each of them?

- What are some aspects of my experience or personality that are unique to me?

- In what settings / pursuits have I received compliments from others?

- What professions have I thought about pursuing, especially when I was little?

Be careful not to discount the importance of this exercise even though it's brief. Often, your first instinct—your gut reaction—will be right on.

Exercise 2 - Experience Inventory

Step 1: Begin by listing significant experiences you have had. They can be positive or negative. Write them down in the first column. This should take about fifteen to twenty minutes. Don't limit your thinking. Let your mind flow, and brainstorm as many experiences as you can think of in your life. Don't worry about whether they are important enough to be included at this point, just get them down. Think about experiences that have shaped who you are: it could be jobs, school projects, sports or musical instruments you played, specific classes, trips you have taken or even things you have done with your family and friends that stand out.

Step 2: Once you have the list, go through each experience and write an L for Life-Giving or a T for Transformational (the definitions are below). Realize that not every experience on your list will have a T or an L next to it. Here is a little more explanation about the codes:

Life-Giving (L)—This experience or task brought life to you. When you finished this activity, you had more energy than when you started and you would really enjoy doing this activity or event again and again. You would probably do it for free because you like it so much. An example of this in my own life is playing the piano. I enjoy it and feel more energy after I have played, even though I am not that good. I would encourage you not to make these items directly related to work. As you list them, your mind will work through trends and connections. For example, although I do not have as much time as I would like to play the piano now, I have been able to participate on the board for our city's symphony orchestra. It is a great connection point with other leaders and is close to something I enjoy.

Transformational (T)—These experiences were ones that were hard and challenging but that you saw good come out of. They helped shape who you have become. You may not have enjoyed going through it, but you can see how God has used it in your life and in those around you. An example of a transformational event for me was my first job out of college. I was an internal sales rep for a technology company and had to make 100 cold calls every day. I hated it. But it was transformational as I learned that I wanted to work for a smaller company and that really good customer service is all about being able to surpass your clients' expectations—to under promise and over deliver.

When you get finished with this exercise, you will have a number of activities or experiences that were not Life-Giving or Transformational. That is okay. For now, we are not going to worry about those.

Step 3: Look at the Life-Giving activities and think through why each activity was Life-Giving for you. What was your role in those experiences that made you come alive?

Delivering *Your* Future

For example, you may have had a group project you enjoyed. As you think through the experience, you may realize that you derived energy from identifying participants for the group. You would then list that as the action you took that made it significant: finding people for the team. Or perhaps you were asked or assigned to be on the group, but you were the one who pulled everyone's work together at the end for the final deliverable. You would list your role as following through to completion. Or maybe you wrote an individual section and you enjoyed looking through resources to find the data. You would then list your role as research.

Step 4: Now read through the transformational experiences. This will undoubtedly be harder to do, and the important thing is to push through to identify the learning that resulted from the experience. You may feel a lot of emotions as you work through this list and that is okay. Let yourself feel it and reflect on it as this will allow you to get to the core of the experience. An example of a transformational experience could be not making a soccer team. Think through why it did not work and what your role was in that failure. For example, you might realize that in order to make the soccer team, you would have given up a number of other activities that were important to you—like spending time with your family or playing other sports. The learning would be that you like quality time with your family or that you like variety in your daily experiences.

Step 5: Now pull out the statements that you wrote down and create a list. Try to pull out themes. You might notice that you enjoy completing tasks or finishing something once it is started. You like to have the rules and guidelines laid out and then follow them completely. Or you may come alive when you have freedom to be creative. This list should complement the answers you wrote in the first exercise. Once you have done this, try and narrow it down to the top five themes that seem to be significant for you.

Hearing about Your Gifting

As I talked about a few chapters back, God intended us to live in community. We cannot do it alone and we're not intended to. Other people may be able to speak into your gifting and help you identify it in a way you cannot. Recently, I was blessed by a good friend in this way. He was making an introduction for me to someone else and he described me as one of the most intentional guys he knows. In a simple way, he affirmed one of my core gifts of discernment and the way I use it to bless others. His words blessed me and spoke truth into my life.

Hopefully, in your family you have people who are able to give you insights into your strengths in a way that is impactful but, if not, perhaps there are friends, teachers and mentors who can step in as well. Think through the people in your life who are effective in forgetting about themselves and who really seek to understand you.

Exercise 3 - Ask People You Trust

Reach out to three of these people. You can certainly pick some people who are your age, but I would encourage you to reach out to some who are older than you and have more life perspective and experience. Have them think through the following questions:

- What do you see as my core strengths? When, specifically, have you seen them?

- What industries or professions do you think they could be used in?

- Do you know anyone who could help me learn about these areas or provide connections?

This exercise works best if the people you are close to can do this and then actually get together with you to review what they have generated. It will have more impact and you will remember it more if they actually walk you through it. Again, once you have completed this, try to narrow it down to five to seven things that you are consistently hearing from multiple people. Invite God into this space to help guide and direct you as you think through it.

Exercise 4 - Complete Personality Tests

There are a lot of personality tests out there that can help provide a pretty objective description of your gifting, but there are three that I have found to be especially useful.

Clifton Strengths—Narrow Down Specific Skills

Clifton Strengths is one that is widely used and has helped a lot of people narrow in on their gifting. It is very specific in defining core areas of skill, although there are certainly other personality/inventory tests that accomplish similar objectives.

DISC—Confirm the Way You Are Wired Up

The DISC profile will help you get at how you are wired up and provide insight into the type of environment / job that would complement your skill set. For example, if you are a high D you need to position yourself in an environment that allows you to either lead others or lead yourself. Or if you are a high C, find an industry that is highly regulated and requires specific expertise and oversight.

Kolbe—Identify Your Approach to Solving Problems

The third test I have found beneficial is the Kolbe. The Kolbe will help you understand how to work better in team settings, because it tells you how you approach problems. If you are a high Fact Finder and you are confronted with a problem, you will gravitate toward research and seeking an array of options to help you. Or if you are a Quick Start, you will jump in and just try things to see if they will work.

These three tests will provide you with a fairly thorough understanding of yourself, and they are all relatively quick to take—around thirty minutes or less.

By now, you probably have a pretty good list of skills going. When you have a lot of options, you can also have a lot of confusion, so now you have the hard work of boiling it down. Try to get your list of giftings down to three to five that you are really good at and that make you come alive. Keep in mind, this does not have to be perfect. I love this quote from C. S. Lewis's *The Screwtape Letters* about believing in your talents. The narrator of the book is one demon who is advising another demon, and so when he talks about the "Enemy" he is really talking about God:

The Enemy wants to bring the man to a state of mind in which
he could design the best cathedral in the world, and know it to be
the best, and rejoice in the fact, without being any more (or less)
or otherwise glad at having done it than he would be if it had
been done by another. The Enemy wants him, in the end, to be so
free from any bias in his own favor that he can rejoice in his own
talents as frankly and gratefully as in his neighbors' talents—or
in a sunrise, an elephant or a waterfall. He wants each man, in
the long run, to be able to recognize all creatures (even himself)
as glorious and excellent things.[3]

Discussion / Reflection Questions

1. If you haven't already completed the steps in this chapter, when do you plan to make time to do so?

2. Where is a place you can go that is without distraction?

3. How did you see God show up in the process of working through them?

Chapter 20

Explore the Context

All vocations are intended by God to manifest His love in the world.

Thomas Merton

College can be a lot of fun, but after four, or maybe five years, it does end and you will need to find a job. But if you have an accurate idea of your gifting, it really is not that bad. If you find your sweet spot, you will enjoy what you are doing and feel like you are alive when you do it.

As you start to think about a full-time vocation, a good thing to remember is that God created work before the fall. Genesis 2:15, 19-20 says:

> The Lord God took the man and put him in the Garden of Eden to work it and take care of it. … Now the Lord God had formed out of the ground all the wild animals and all the birds in the sky. He brought them to the man to see what he would name them; and whatever the man called each living creature, that was its name. So the man gave names to all the livestock, the birds in the sky and all the wild animals.

Delivering *Your* Future

Did you catch that? Adam is working directly with God to tend to the garden and name all the animals. What a job! Talk about an outstanding direct supervisor. It could not get much better. But it did not last. Adam and Eve sinned against God and separated themselves from his work. They fell hard. As Genesis 3:17-19 shows, work got harder for them:

> Cursed is the ground because of you; through painful toil you will
>
> eat food from it all the days of your life. It will produce thorns and
>
> thistles for you, and you will eat the plants of the field. By the sweat
>
> of your brow you will eat your food (NIV).

Yet in spite of this, the Bible is full of people living out their gifting in their vocations: Joseph leading Egypt; John the Baptist proclaiming the crazy message that the Savior was coming; Paul using his keen intellect to encourage many about faith. Tom Nelson wrote a good examination of the importance of work. In *Work Matters* he takes some time to develop Dorothy Sayers's point that "the First Adam was cursed with labor and suffering; the redemption of labor and suffering is the triumph of the second Adam— the Carpenter nailed to the cross."[1] Christ has atoned for our sin in the Garden of Eden, and now our work will lead toward the day when he will make all things right. As we live in the in-between period—after Christ's resurrection but before his return—our work needs to point people to God. Nelson suggests the following:

> A large stewardship of our calling in the workplace is faithfully
>
> showing up every day and demonstrating to others around us
>
> our good in and through our work. Seeking to live out a faithful
>
> presence in our workplaces means that we incarnate the gospel by

doing good work and being exemplary workers. It means that we extend common grace to our coworkers and our customers and seek their good. As image-bearers of God, who is a worker, we must remember that our work has intrinsic value in itself and is to be an act of worship. We also must grasp that our work has instrumental value in that it provides for economic needs, allows us to care for the needs of others, and creates a sphere of influence for the gospel to be lived out and shared.[2]

God is going to use you after college in a vocation, or multiple vocations, to bring Him glory and to influence others around you. In the last chapter, we explored how you are wired up. Now let's look at the context in which you could use those skills. Below are a few exercises to help you get at the context of your gifting.

Exercise 5 - Brainstorm

Set a timer for five minutes. When you start the timer begin to write down any people or companies that have impressed you. Also jot down any industries you have thought you might want to go into in the past. Don't limit yourself: it could be anything from the shoes you wear to a teacher who was especially influential at one point in your life. After you have done this, pick the top five from the list.

Exercise 6 - Triage Your Thinking

Once you've picked your top five people or companies, list your top skills that you think you could use next to them. Rank each area based on your skill. For example, you may have identified that you always have admired a neurologist who lives in your neighborhood. List his or her name and profession in the first spot and then list your gifting next. Your skills might be listening, analyzing data and writing. Now rank each of your skills alongside of this profession on a scale of 1-5 with 5 being best, based on what you know about the profession. Certainly listening would be important and useful if you were a neurologist, so you would rank that as a 5. Analyzing data is probably less important in this role, so you might rank that a 3, and writing would have very little to do with your success as a neurologist, so rank that a 2. That would give you a combined score of 10 out of 15 for that area. Go through and do this for each of the areas you are involved in. Once this is completed take the top five scores. Next, take some time to read about that profession or company online, so that you know some of the basic vernacular and people who are involved.

Exercise 7 - Connecting

Now see if you can make a connection with someone who is in that profession or research online to learn about the company. You should also pull any connections that were provided to you in the previous exercise when you reached out to people you admired and asked them about your gifting. Most people remember what it was like to be a young adult trying to figure out a direction in life and will be willing to give you some of their time. Find a way to connect with them via social media or through someone you know and try and schedule a time to talk with them and learn from them. You can keep it really simple when you reach out to them. Tell them something like this:

John Smith recommend that I connect with you (or whatever the connection point is with that person). I am about to graduate from _____ high school and will be attending _____ college in the fall. I admire you and what you do (or you have always had a passion for the company). It would be an incredible encouragement to me if you would give me thirty minutes of your time to help me learn more about the profession.

Then provide them with three specific options of when you are available. Many people err at this point by suggesting that they can meet whenever the other person wants to. When you get this kind of a request and your life is packed, the idea of looking at a calendar often delays a response. Narrowing it down for them will help you get a quicker response.

When you get the interview set up, make sure that you spend at least thirty minutes preparing for it. Look at their bio online and jot down a few questions about their company or industry. This will help you feel more prepared going into the meeting and allow you to be more present while you are there. Always include this question at the end of your time: "Do you know of anyone else I should talk with?" Often a connection of a connection can lead you to the best results.

Make sure you arrive a few minutes early for the meeting. I heard a speaker give the analogy once of a jet pilot. The best jet pilots in the world think through their flight before they start. They visualize the take-off, possible complications and the destination. Then they go for it. The flight is more successful if they have taken the time to see how it will happen in their minds. You can apply the same thing before the interview. Take a few minutes right before you go in to pray through each stage of the meeting. Ask God to give you a strong awareness of His will during the conversation and answer the question: *What is the best outcome of this meeting?* This will help you to engage more while you are with the person.

Once you have completed the meeting, take fifteen minutes to summarize the most valuable things you learned. Review your notes, highlight, type up a summary or do a voice recording about what you learned. By doing this, you will lock it in your long-term memory, and it will start to change your behavior and influence your thinking. Make sure you send an email or handwritten thank-you note within twenty-four hours of the meeting, and that you keep track of anyone else that the person recommended you meet with. After you meet with someone they recommended, loop back to the original person and thank them again for the connection.

On a side note, be open for opportunities that are actually part of your education as well. When I was at Dartmouth, I was able to do an independent study focused on serving the over fifty-five market. It was helpful because it allowed me to better understand the landscape, forced me to connect with opportunities, provided a lot of accountability to get something done instead of just talking about it, and it ultimately led me to two of the companies that have been acquired. You will have to look for niches in the educational system to create these opportunities, but it is well worth it, as these opportunities can often be more valuable than classroom learning.

Exercise 8 - Identifying Steps

After meeting people and experiencing five of the areas you identified, it will be important to think of at least the first three steps needed to get you into that profession. Take it back to the most basic level and build from there. For example, if you want to build a real estate development company the steps could be:

1. Buy a rental property to manage while you are in college.

2. Prove that it can cash flow, borrow against it, and do it again.

3. Take real estate classes in school.

4. Find jobs/internships that allow you to gain experience in the space.

5. Build relationships with individuals and banks (real estate takes capital).

6. Write your plan and recruit someone you have met along the way to help.

Think through how much time you will take at each point and keep in mind that careers are rarely linear. They take turns and have unexpected events, but having an idea of how to get there will be helpful. Also, some professions really do take years of schooling and preparation to get into. If you see yourself going down one of those paths, it will be important to lay that out in advance.

The important thing to realize and appreciate is that you often have to work your way through steps. Don't be discouraged if the first few steps or roles are not as glamorous as you might like them to be. Stay humble and teachable and try to bring glory to God in whatever role you find yourself in. As Martin Luther King, Jr. said: "If it falls to your lot to be a street sweeper, sweep the streets like Michelangelo painted pictures, like Shakespeare wrote poetry, like Beethoven composed music; sweep streets so well that all the host of Heaven and earth will have to pause and say, 'Here lived a great street sweeper, who swept his job well.'"3

Discussion / Reflection Questions

1. Have you looked at the guides at the back of this book?

2. What are some of the things that might be stopping you from reaching out to someone you respect or applying for a job or internship you might want?

3. Who can help motivate you to invest the time in this important work even though it might not feel very urgent? Would it help them to work through them as well? Reach out to them now and tell them what you are working on to help ensure you get it across the line.

Chapter 21

Trust God for the Elusive Future

By all means, make plans for your future. Write goals and dreams.
Just make sure you write them in pencil so that you can erase them if
God changes your direction.

Dr. Ramesh Richard

The time has finally come. You wrapped up your last summer at home, said goodbye to your friends and drove to college full of hopes, dreams and expectations. It is both exciting and gut-wrenching. So much work, planning and effort went into getting you to this point.

The first few weeks are exhilarating—the rush of figuring out all things new, being able to really determine your own schedule and routines, working to figure out friends and signing up for clubs and activities. Then classes start and you realize how hard it is going to be. You may have moments of wondering if you are going to be able to do it or questioning whether you picked the right college. With the help of those around you, you will work through it step by step.

After you get through these emotions, another task will loom in front of you: What are you going to do next? What is the point of all of this education? That's right. The best colleges start you thinking about this really quickly, because the sooner you start to think about it, the sooner you will start to figure it out. And guess what? They really do want you to figure out what you will do after college and how you will do it because they have summer internship statistics to hit, and of course the ultimate measure of a college's success—placement upon graduation. If they can get you to obsess about it early on—to start taking interviews, leveraging your network and learning about things that interest you, then there is a more certain chance that you will land where you are supposed to be, right? Well, right in some aspects but wrong in others.

Jesus told us in John 10:10 that "the thief comes only to steal and kill and destroy; I came that they may have life, and have it abundantly." God wants you to have full, abundant life even in college. He has work for you to do and people for you to impact in the present, and if you live in a constant state of worry about the future, you will miss out on the work he has planned for you right now. So how do you overcome this temptation to live in the future and instead live authentically in the present in spite of the pressure?

Believe God Is for You and Your Future

The only way to not be carried off by the whims and worries about your future is to believe that God is for you. That is what makes the Christian faith so different from other religions—we believe that, because of Jesus, God is already for us, that we don't have to work to earn it. Christ paid the penalty, he took on your sins and requires us only to accept this and believe. God has done it all. He sees you, understands you and accepts you with all your shortcomings and failings. He has a plan for you and for your future. Paul emphasized this idea in his seminal chapter on our relationship with God in Romans 8:28:"And we know that God causes all things to work together for good to those who love God, to those who are called according to His purpose." You have been called. God is at work in your life to will and to act according to His desires. He will not abandon you to a hopeless future or leave you alone in what is to come. This verse does not mean that it won't be hard or that every situation will work out perfectly, but you have to believe that in the end, God is working to will and act in your life according to His good purposes, even if you do not see them until after this life is over.

David says something similar in Psalm 139. He speaks directly of how God created each one of us. David tells us that, "My frame was not hidden from you when I was made in the secret place, when I was woven together in the depths of the earth. Your eyes saw my unformed body; all the days ordained for me were written in your book before one of them came to be" (Psalm 139:15-16, NIV). Draw comfort and encouragement from this. God knew where you would be as you read this book, knew where you would go to college, and He knows all that's in store for you during your college years. He knew it before the world began. Nothing is a surprise to Him and He has a plan and purpose for all your days.

But Christ realized this would be a challenge for us—trusting in God for the future rather than worrying about it. He spoke directly about it in Matthew 6:

> For this reason I say to you, do not be worried about your life, as to
> what you will eat or what you will drink; nor for your body, as to
> what you will put on. Is not life more than food, and the body more
> than clothing? Look at the birds of the air, that they do not sow, nor
> reap nor gather into barns, and yet your heavenly Father feeds them.
> Are you not worth much more than they? And who of you by being
> worried can add a single hour to his life? And why are you worried
> about clothing? Observe how the lilies of the field grow; they do not
> toil nor do they spin, yet I say to you that not even Solomon in all

his glory clothed himself like one of these. But if God so clothes the grass of the field, which is alive today and tomorrow is thrown into the furnace, will He not much more clothe you? You of little faith! Do not worry then, saying, 'What will we eat?' or 'What will we drink?' or 'What will we wear for clothing?' For the Gentiles eagerly seek all these things; for your heavenly Father knows that you need all these things. But seek first His kingdom and His righteousness, and all these things will be added to you (Matthew 6:25–33).

At one point in my life, I was really worried about purchasing an investment property. It was going to require significant resources from funds we had worked hard to save up and it was in an area of real estate that was somewhat new to me. We were not sure about how our investment would play out—there was a chance we could lose and lose big. Even if a wise risk, it was still a risk. As I was wrestling with it in my mind, I remember walking out of our office and noticing a tree filled with bright red berries and a flock of birds eating away at the berries. It was the dead of winter. There were very few signs of life at that time of year, yet God provided a feast for those birds. There are times in your life when you seem to be more spiritually aware, when God makes the veil thinner between heaven and earth. This was one of those times for me. It was as if the images of the birds were clearer, their chirping sharper than it normally was and God was raising my awareness to get my attention. In that moment, Matthew 6 came to my mind: *Look at the birds of the air, that they do not sow, nor reap nor gather into barns, and yet your heavenly Father feeds them.* I was treating my resources like they were mine, as if I owned them and could direct them. The truth was that God had always provided for me and would continue to do so. By worrying about the future and second-guessing His leading, I was showing my lack of faith in God, who controls the universe and provides for every living thing.

214

Not worrying about the future starts with trusting in God for today and for tomorrow. Trust that He has taken care of men and women for generations and He is not going to overlook you.

Hold It Loosely

It is easy to get caught up in an idealistic view of the future, to become almost obsessed with trying to make it happen or align with what we need. I found myself in that position when I was at Vanderbilt. I felt pressure to get straight A's and to set myself up for a stellar consulting job in Atlanta. The pressure became too much for me. I had my hand wrapped around this ideal so tightly that God had to figuratively pry it away from my grip, finger by finger.

Proverbs 16:9 says, "The heart of a man plans his way. But the Lord directs his steps." Notice this verse sets up a two-step dichotomy. We need to plan and prepare for the future, but we are not ultimately in control of it—God is the one who directs our steps. Our human nature wants to plan the way and control our steps. It is hard for us to give up the control and trust God to guide us along the journey, but He asks us to. God's timing is not our own and that can become very frustrating, but that uncertainty is exactly what He is asking us to trust Him with. If God did everything our way, then trusting Him wouldn't require faith, only a willingness to delegate.

I thought I would be in business school within three years of finishing my undergraduate degree. After all, that was what most people did because it was the smart thing to do. Instead, God took me to seminary in Dallas and then to work with my family's company for five years in Indianapolis. When I finally arrived at business school on the east coast, I was one of the oldest in my class. It felt kind of awkward at first, but it actually worked out better in hindsight. I had more life experience to bring to my graduate studies, which helped me to keep everything in perspective in a way that I could not have done right after completing my undergraduate program. It also created an amazing window of time for our family—a two-year period when we could engage with each other in a way we could not with the normal "noise" of life around us. Our kids were young and there was a lot of time spent playing on the floor or following them around as they explored the world and developed their own words. We left the pressures and obligations of a town where we had roots and connections and enjoyed a sweet time of learning and leaning into our nuclear family. We went skiing together often and had movie night together every Friday—the warm feeling of gathering on the couch while the wind howled outside started to feel almost sacred. As we look back on those years, we realize how hard they were and yet how transformational they were for our family. We would not trade them for anything, even though they were not part of the original playbook I had set out.

Catching the Wind: A Vision for What Is Next

If you have ever been sailing, you know the wind can absolutely make or break your experience. When you catch a strong wind and the sail billows outward, it is a thrill to lean out over the hull with the water gliding along beneath you. It helps maximize your speed and keeps the boat from capsizing, but there is also something humbling about being connected to that kind of power—a thing so utterly outside of your control. But to experience and leverage this kind of force, first you have to find the wind. Every experienced sailor has a way to do it. Some look at the leaves on the trees, some hold their fingers up in the wind, some listen for it, and some are just experienced enough to feel it on their faces. Whatever the method, once they find it they go with it. That is what the last few chapters have been about: finding the wind by identifying the way you are gifted and some of the initial contexts that will allow you to use it. Once you find that gifting and the way to stay in it, you will be able to lean into the wind and really sail.

You will find that if you write down where you want to go, it will be amazing how you will start to naturally work toward getting there. Here are some questions to help get you started:

- Where do you ideally want to live?
- What type of income level do you think you need?
- What does your day-to-day work look like? In an office or elsewhere?

Another exercise that will help you is to take a blank sheet of paper and write down what you ideally want life to look like in three years. One of my mentors, who started and leads an investment group with over $23 billion in assets under advisement, encouraged me with these words: "I have learned in life that I almost always have to think and even talk five years ahead of where I am presently. If not, I may never get there." Be specific about where you want to go. Talk about what you want your life to look like spiritually, relationally, vocationally, mentally and physically. Write it out in a narrative format so it can become real. Again, limit yourself to one page and give yourself about ten minutes to do it.

Most people want to have someone tell them what they should do. We want God to tell us the playbook so we can just follow it. But God did not intend it to be that way. Think about how he announced Christ's birth to the shepherds. It was just an ordinary night and they were tending their flock like any other night. They were not given warning or advanced notice. God showed up and transformed their lives forever while they were just doing the same work they did every day. Seek out God's leading along the way and step in confidence when you see him move in your life—don't second guess. When you feel the wind, make your preparations and then follow.

Delivering *Your* Future

1. Based on this chapter, how can you avoid getting carried away by the whims and worries about your future?

2. Think of a time in your life when you clearly saw a picture of God's providence, either in your life or elsewhere. How can you use this image as a reminder of God's faithfulness?

3. Take 3-5 minutes and brainstorm what you think your life will look like in five years. Don't limit yourself with any categories — jot down your age in five years and start creating some ideas about what it will look like.

Chapter 22

Finding Hope in College

In a desperate world where people look to anything else and everything else to satisfy them, God wants you to find satisfaction in Him. The idols, siren's songs and mirages of accomplishments, pleasing people, indulgences and your own image will come at you hard during college. The enemy will do everything in his power to get you to live for one of these gods rather than the true and living God. They are ridiculously alluring. Don't be deceived into thinking that what you see in the material world is all there is. As Paul reminds us, "our struggle is not against flesh and blood, but against the rulers, against the powers, against the world forces of this darkness, against the spiritual forces of wickedness in the heavenly places" (Ephesians 6:12). There is a war going on in the spiritual realms for your soul and the next few years are going to be pivotal in shaping the course of your life.

How do you think God will react to your time in college? It is easy to picture God looking down with a stern expression, judging your every move and hoping you will step it up. While his heart is certainly saddened by sin and waywardness, still he takes great delight in you. You were His idea after all. He smiles when He thinks about you. The Bible says that God rejoices over us—He even sings over us (Zephaniah 3:17). It's a little bit like that John Legend song: "'Cause all of me loves all of you." Is that how you think of God's love for you? You should.

We have talked about a lot of techniques and principles to help you approach the next few years. Such as, how important it is to run after Christ with all your strength, soul and mind. Or to think about balance in your life and the people who surround you, those who will walk alongside you. We've talked about doing the hard work of uncovering your gifting while also leaning into Christ for the future. God wants people to live stout-heartedly for Him. You will be one of them. Hard times will come, to be sure. I don't say this to be cynical or morbid. It is simply a reality of life in a fallen world. Job 5:7 says, "for man is born to trouble, as sparks fly upward." But the good news is that God has promised to never leave you or forsake you (Hebrews 13:5). Neither will He allow you to be tempted beyond what you can bear (1 Corinthians 10:13). So don't be surprised when troubles come—when lust seems really strong or loneliness discourages you and overwhelms your spirit. When you have the strong temptation to numb yourself with drink, food and entertainment even though all you should really do is listen to that song that makes you cry and helps you get in touch with your emotions.

During some of my darkest hours in college, when I could not see the light and could not understand how God could possibly use me for His glory, I started seeing a counselor. Her name was Marilyn Ryerson and she must have been at least sixty at the time. She lived in a historic farmhouse that seemed to have been swallowed up by the city around it. One particular day stands out in my mind. When I turned into her driveway off one of the busiest thoroughfares in the city, I could suddenly feel that I had entered a different place. Rather than the pavement and potholes of the city, loose gravel hit my tires. I was aware of the sounds and smells as I walked up—the creak of the old boards on her porch, the weathered doorbell slightly golden from frequent visitors. When I entered her parlor—because that was the only way to describe the room— time seemed to cease. I could hear a clock ticking from somewhere in the room, and I took in the musty smell of things well-used and well-loved. Marilyn seemed to always give her clients a few minutes to sit in the space to allow for some solitude and resetting from the hurried world around.

She came in and greeted me with a hug. At almost six feet tall, I always felt like I towered over her five-foot frame, especially during the hug part. After listening to me and all of the challenges I was walking through, she looked at me and made a very simple suggestion: two words that have stuck with me ever since. "Stay present," she said. She explained that it was a concept from Alcoholics Anonymous. After all, we are all addicted to something, even if it is not as extreme as alcohol. She explained that when you are tempted to take the next drink, when it seems to be an all-consuming desire, it can be overwhelming to think about staying dry for an entire day or even an afternoon. So the way to take the pressure off is to focus on staying present with Christ right now in this very moment. Don't worry about tomorrow or next week. Just be mindful with Christ where you are at. The principle resonated with me a great deal. I could hear the spiritual undertones: something about not worrying about tomorrow and abiding in Him ...

Marilyn's admonition to stay present followed me through a number of circumstances: when I wanted to run from accountability and discipline in college; when I wanted to quit my first job after making eighty cold calls in three hours; when our kids were little and I frequently found myself lying next to them in our playroom feeling so tired and overwhelmed by all we had to do that I either wanted to sleep or just start getting things done. I certainly did not want to stay in that playroom and press the same button on the plastic piano and listen to the same melody for the hundredth time. Those words follow me even now, when I find myself meeting with a client or the president of a company and my mind starts to wander. *Stay present*, I hear her say. *Ask God for his presence in the moment to minister to the person you are with in a real way.*

Robert J. Hastings wrote a short essay that drives home the importance of staying engaged. If you stay present with it and take his words in, I think you will be pleasantly surprised.

Delivering *Your* Future

The Station

Tucked away in our subconscious is an idyllic vision. We see ourselves on a long trip that spans the continent. We are traveling by train. Out the windows we drink in the passing scene of cars on nearby highways, of children waving at a crossing, of cattle grazing on a distant hillside, of smoke pouring from a power plant, of row upon row of corn and wheat, of flatlands and valleys, of mountains and rolling hillsides, of city skylines and village halls.

But uppermost in our minds is the final destination. On a certain day at a certain hour we will pull into the station. Bands will be playing and flags waving. Once we get there so many wonderful dreams will come true, and the pieces of our lives will fit together like a completed jigsaw puzzle. How restlessly we pace the aisles, damning the minutes for loitering—waiting, waiting, waiting for the station.

"When we reach the station, that will be it!" We cry.

"When I'm 18."

"When I buy a new 450SL Mercedes Benz!"

"When I put the last kid through college."

"When I have paid off the mortgage!"

"When I get a promotion."

"When I reach the age of retirement, I shall live happily ever after!"

Sooner or later we must realize there is no station, no one place to arrive at once and for all. The true joy of life is the trip. The station is only a dream. It constantly outdistances us.

"Relish the moment" is a good motto, especially when coupled with
Psalm 118:24: "This is the day which the Lord hath made; we will
rejoice and be glad in it." It isn't the burdens of today that drive men
mad. It is the regrets over yesterday and the fear of tomorrow. Regret
and fear are twin thieves who rob us of today.

So stop pacing the aisles and counting the miles. Instead, climb more
mountains, eat more ice cream, go barefoot more often, swim more
rivers, watch more sunsets, laugh more, cry less. Life must be lived as
we go along. The station will come soon enough.[1]

Stay Present in your college experience. Allow yourself to feel the highs and the lows that will inevitably come. Lock arms with some fellow sojourners who can help you fully embrace the love of God. Take courage. Rest in Christ's hope. Live Abundantly in College. You already have what it takes.

Discussion / Reflection Questions

1. How can the concept of "staying present" help you when you feel tempted or tired or weak?

2. How can you take courage from the knowledge that God has already given you all that you need?

3. Take a moment to pray that God will fill you with his Spirit and that He will use your college experience for good. Enjoy His presence right now in this moment.

Notes

Introduction

1. C. S. Lewis, *The Silver Chair,* (Chorley, United Kingdom: Geoffrey Bles, 1953).

2. Greg Lukianoff & Jonathan Haidt, *The Coddling of the American Mind* (London, England: Penguin Press, 2018).

3. Ceylan Yeginsu, "U.K. Appoints Minister for Loneliness", *The New York Time,* January 7, 2018, https://www.nytimes.com/2018/01/17/world/europe/uk-britain-loneliness.html.

Chapter 2: Owning a Piece of You

1. John Ortberg, *Soul Keeping: Caring For the Most Important Part of You* (Grand Rapids, MI: Zondervan, 2014).

2. Andy Crouch, *Playing God: Redeeming the Gift of Power* (Downers Grove, IL: Intervarsity Press, 2013).

3. Ibid.

Chapter 3: People Pleasing

1. Walt Disney, *Saving Mr. Banks,* 2013.

2. Bob Goff, *Love Does: Discover a Secretly Incredible Life in an Ordinary World* (Nashville, TN: Thomas Nelson, 2012), Chapter 4.

3. C. S. Lewis, *Screwtape Letters* (New York, NY: HarperCollins, 1942), 57.

4. Proverbs 13:20, New American Standard Bible.

Chapter 5: Your Achievements

1. Bob Goff, Speech Given on May 4, 2016, Indianapolis, IN.

Chapter 6: Your Indulgences

Delivering *Your* Future

1. Charles Swindoll, *David: A Man of Passion and Destiny* (Nashville, TN: W Publishing Group, 1997) 182.

Chapter 7: Your Body Image

1. Timothy Keller, *David and Bathsheba* (Gospel in Life, 08/23/09) https://gospelinlife.com/downloads/david-and-bathsheba-6017/

2. C. S. Lewis, *Screwtape Letters* (New York, NY: HarperCollins, 1803), 77.

3. Elizabeth Saviteer, Yasemin Merwede, Françoise Vermeylen, Jaina Teeluck, and Chuck Eng, "Collegiate survey project" (https://www.nationaleatingdisorders.org/CollegiateSurveyProject, 2011)

4. https://www.ncbi.nlm.nih.gov/pmc/articles/PMC3721327/

5. Suzanne Collins, *The Hunger Games*, (New York, NY: Scholastic Press, 2008).

Chapter 8: The Mirage

1. Susan Snyder, "Addressing Suicide Among College Students," http://www.nbcphiladelphia.com/news/local/Addressing-Suicide-Among-College-Students-245739971.html#ixzz3ZxLwNTtQ

2. John Ortberg, *Soul Keeping: Caring For the Most Important Part of You* (Grand Rapids, MI: Zondervan, 2014), 23.

3. C. S. Lewis, *Mere Christianity* (Chorley, United Kingdom: Geoffrey Bles, 1952), 198.

Chapter 9: Illustrated Hope

1. Lois Lowry, *The Giver* (New York: Laurel-Leaf, 1993).

2. C. S. Lewis, *The Lion, the Witch and the Wardrobe* (Chorley, United Kingdom: Geoffrey Bles, 1950).

Chapter 10: Grounded Hope

1. Genesis 3:15.

2. Bob Deffinbaugh, "*Abraham's Call and God's Covenant,*" https://bible.org/seriespage/5-abrahams-call-and-gods-covenant-genesis-1126-1727

3. Genesis 39:2.

4. Genesis 45:7-8.

5. Edward Mote, *My Hope is Built*, 1843.

Chapter 11: Believe in Christ

1. Romans 3:23, emphasis added.

2. Max Lucado, *In the Grip of Grace* (Cleveland, OH: Word Publishing, 1996), 39-40.

3. Chapell, Bryan. *Holiness by Grace: Delighting in the Joy That Is Our Strength* (Wheaton IL: Crossway, 2001) as quoted in Nancy Fitzgerald, *Unanswered, Smoke, Mirrors and God* (San Clemente, CA: Cross Section, 2014), 25.

Chapter 12: Pursue the Father

1. Charles R. Swindoll, *Paul: A Man of Grace and Grit* (Nashville, TN: Thomas Nelson, 2011), iBooks.

2. https://blackaby.org/experiencing-god/

3. Jim Collins, *Good to Great* (New York City, NY: Harper Business, 2001).

4. Eric Metaxas, *Seven Women* (Nashville: Thomas Nelson, 2015).

5. Andy Crouch, *Playing God: Redeeming the Gift of Power* (Downers Grove, IL: Intervarsity Press, 2013), 117.

6. Ibid, 124.

7. Henri J. M. Nouwen, *Reaching Out: The Three Movements of the Spiritual Life* (New York, NY: Doubleday, 1975), 38.

Chapter 13: Seek Out the Spirit

1. www.frederickbuechner.com/listening-to-your-life/

2. Ibid.

3. https://www.goodreads.com/author/quotes/32106.Fred_Rogers

4. Brennan Manning, *The Ragamuffin Gospel: Good News for the Bedraggled, Beat-Up, and Burnt Out* (Colorado Springs, CO: Multnomah, 2005), 85.

Chapter 14: Making Hope Practical

Delivering *Your* Future

1. Charles Swindoll, quoted in a Conversation on 10/21/2019.

Chapter 15: Create Balance

1. Timothy Keller, The *Reason for God: Belief in an Age of Skepticism*, (New York, NY: Riverhead Books, 2008), 168.

2. Mark Vroegop in a sermon on March 11, 2018. © College Park Church, Indianapolis, IN, www.yourchurch.com

3. Stephen Covey, *The Seven Habits of Highly Effective People* (Glencoe, IL: Free Press 1989).

Chapter 16: Lock Arms

1. Alexander Dumas, *The Man in the Iron Mask* (Knoxville, TN: Wordsworth Classics, 2011).

2. John Hannah, Lecture in Dallas, TX, November 2017.

3. John Eldredge, "Your Deepest Question," https://ransomedheart.com/story/real-men/your-deepest-question.

4. C. S. Lewis, *Mere Christianity*, (Chorley, United Kingdom: Geoffrey Bles, 1952).

5. Timothy Keller, *Prodigal God: Recovering the Heart of the Christian Faith* (London, England: Penguin Books, 2011).

6. Henri J. M. Nouwen, *Reaching Out: The Tree Movements of the Spiritual Life* (New York, NY: Doubleday, 1975), 1986.

7. Timothy Keller, *Prodigal God.*

8. Andy Crouch, *Culture Making: Recovering Our Creative Calling* (Downers Grove, IL: Intervarsity Press, 2013).

9. Ibid.

10. https://www.goodreads.com/author/quotes/32106.Fred_Rogers

11. C. S. Lewis, *The Four Loves.* (Chorley, United Kingdom: Geoffrey Bles, 1960).

12. C. S. Lewis, *Mere Christianity*, (Chorley, United Kingdom: Geoffrey Bles, 1952).

13. Ibid.

14. Henri J. M. Nouwen, *Reaching Out: The Tree Movements of the Spiritual Life* (New

York, NY: Doubleday, 1975).

15. https://www.amazon.com/Four-Loves-C-S-Lewis/dp/0156329301

16. Brené Brown, *Braving the Wilderness: The Quest for True Belonging and the Courage to Stand Alone* (New York, NY: Random House, 2017).

17. Steven Schwartz, *Wicked: The Life and Times of the Wicked Witch of the West*, May 28, 2003.

Chapter 17: Lean into Difficulties

1. Dan Sullivan, *Laws of Lifetime Growth*. https://10xtalk.com/84/.

2. https://www.tpcc.org/messages/didnt-see-it-coming-message

3. https://www.staugustine.com/article/20141016/LIFESTYLE/310169936

4. Horatio G. Spafford, *It Is Well With My Soul*, 1873.

Chapter 18: Fight against Lust

1. C. S. Lewis, *Mere Christianity*, (Chorley, United Kingdom: Geoffrey Bles, 1952).

2. Ibid., 96.

3. Timothy Keller, *The Meaning of Marriage: Facing the Complexities of Commitment with the Wisdom of God* (London, England: Penguin Books, 2011), 221.

4. Ibid., 228.

5. Brad Bigney, *Gospel Treason: Betraying the Gospel with Hidden Idols* (Phillipsburg NJ: P & R Publishing, 2012), 160.

6. Ted Dekker, *The Circle Series* (Nashville, TN: Thomas Nelson, 2011).

7. C. S. Lewis, *Mere Christianity*, 101.

8. Timothy Keller, *Prodigal God: Recovering the Heart of the Christian Faith* (London, England: Penguin Books, 2011), 134.

9. C. S. Lewis, *Mere Christianity*, 99.

Chapter 19: Identifying Your Gifting

1. Dan Sullivan, *The Unique Ability Guide*, September 2009.

2. David Rendall, *The Freak Factor: Discovering Uniqueness by Flaunting Weakness* (Charleston, SC: Advantage Media Group, 2015).

3. C. S. Lewis, *Screwtape Letters* (New York, NY: HarperCollins, 1803), 59.

Chapter 20: Explore the Context

1. Tom Nelson, *Work Matters: Connecting Sunday Worship to Monday Work* (Wheaton, IL: Crossway, 2011), 5.

2. Tom Nelson, *Work Matters: Connecting Sunday Worship to Monday Work* (Wheaton, IL: Crossway, 2011), 51, from Dorothy Sayers, "*Vocation in Work*" in *Callings: Twenty Centuries of Christian Wisdom on Vocation,* ed. William C. Placher (Grand Rapids, MI: Eerdmans, 2005), 406.

3. Tom Nelson, *Work Matters,* 60.

Chapter 22: Finding Hope in College

1. Robert J. Hastings, "*The Station*" (Golden Valley, MN: Tristan Publishing, 2003), The original essay appeared in Ann Landers' column on May 17, 1981.

Acknowledgements

Writing a book is most certainly a team effort. Michael Kineman, you helped develop the content and make it relevant for young adults. Kathy Davis, your candid input and wordsmithing were incredible. Liz Odmark, thanks for encouraging my writing in high school and for finding the typos in this book. Jenni Robbins, you created energy and enthusiasm which helped me persevere. Sam Wilson, your creativity and resourcefulness got this across the line.

Thanks also to my mom, Roxy, for reminding me that a lot of people have ideas for books, but very few actually start writing them.

And finally, my lovely wife Sarah, without your listening ear and encouraging spirit, this book would most certainly not have happened.

Thank you, Holy Spirit, for continuing to prompt me to work on this. My prayer is that this book will encourage and challenge many in their journeys to You.

Exercises

Exercise 1 - Insightful Questions

What are my top three strengths & an example of when I have used them?

1.

2.

3.

What are some aspects of my experience or personality that are unique to me?

-

-

-

In what settings / pursuits have I received compliments from others?

-

-

-

What areas or professions have I thought about doing especially when I was little?

1.

2.

3.

Exercise 2 - Experience Inventory

Experience or Event	Life Giving / Transformational	What did you do? What made it significant? What skills did you use?

Top 5 Themes from Experiences

1.

2.

3.

4.

5.

Exercise 3 – Ask People You Trust

Who are 3 people who know me well that would help me with this?

1.

2.

3.

Send the following note to the people you identified:

Dear [NAME], Thanks for being an important part of my life. I respect you and value your input in my life. I am seeking to think and pray through what next steps might look like for me after college and I would really value your help by answering the following questions:

• What do you see as my core strengths? When specifically have you seen me use them?
• What industries or professions do you think they could be used in?
• Do you know anyone who could help me learn about these areas?

Thank you very much for helping me. I greatly appreciate it.

Exercise 4 – Complete Personality Tests

DISC:

Scores	Statement I Most Resonated With
D -	
I –	
S -	
C-	

KOLBE:

Scores	Statement I Most Resonated With
Fact Finder -	
Follow Through -	
Quick Start-	
Implementer -	

Top Strengths from Clifton Strengths:

1.

2.

3.

Exercise 5 – Brainstorm

TOP 5

1.

2.

3.

4.

5.

Exercise 6 – Triage Your Thinking

Area	3 Skills / Talents that Align	Ranking
	_____ _____ _____	_____ _____ Total: ____
	_____ _____ _____	_____ _____ Total: ____
	_____ _____ _____	_____ _____ Total: ____
	_____ _____ _____	_____ _____ Total: ____
	_____ _____ _____	_____ _____ Total: ____

Exercise 7 – Connecting

Area	Connections

Exercise 8 – Identifying Steps

Area	Action Steps
	1. 2. 3.
	1. 2. 3.
	1. 2. 3.

CPSIA information can be obtained
at www.ICGtesting.com
Printed in the USA
LVHW030202050121
675395LV00004B/358